THE HEART AS ORIGAMI

THE HEART AS ORIGAMI

CONTEMPORARY BUDDHIST POETS

Edited by Padmacandra (Pippa Meek),
with *Julia Lewis*
and *Subhadramati*

Rising Fire Press
London 2005

First published 2005 by Rising Fire Press, 22 Approach Road, London E2 9LY
padmacandra@btinternet.com

ISBN 0 9531266 2 5

Book design by Ananda (Stephen Parr): ananda@wolfatthedoor.fsnet.co.uk

Printed in Malta by Progress Press Co Limited, Valletta, VLT 07 MALTA

Imagine you are walking through a meadow of wild grasses and flowers in high summer. Wherever you look, there is a profusion of diverse plant life, all suffused with the radiant gold of the sun. Even if one was to concentrate on one square foot of the whole field, the variety, beauty and sheer quantity of different shapes, colours and fragrances would be amazing.

Likewise this book represents a very small section of the whole wide and exciting field of Buddhist poets and writers practising their craft in, or translated into, English today – which at its best is suffused with the golden light of Buddhist practice.

One of our aims was to create a work which was poem rather than poet led, and in which there was both a sense of the uniqueness of each piece of writing, and the interconnectedness of each individual part. We desired that the qualities of Dharma practice should shine through the writing, not necessarily in terms of the subject matter of the poems, but through their awakeness and spontaneity.

There is already a rich strand in the ancestry of poetry that comes directly out of the experiences of Buddhist practitioners throughout the ages. This is especially true of poetry from Japan, China and India (7th century onwards), and nowadays in Northern America.

Both poetry and the Dharma tend towards metaphorical truth as opposed to dogma – to cultivating the qualities needed to remain steady in the face of seeming uncertainties. This goes towards explaining the affinities found between the two forms of practice. Indeed, they are not essentially separate activities. The meditative and ethical practices undertaken by Buddhists aim to develop those very qualities that are essential for the creative process; openness of heart, appreciative awareness, alertness, clarity, and the capacity to sustain concentration or presence. These are above all necessary for the poetic, Dharmic, and essentially human task of 'bearing witness' – of being willing and able to bear witness with clarity and emotional positivity, to the myriad sublime, ordinary and terrifying phenomena of our lives, and the lives of others; of the transience, sorrow and exquisite beauty of life.

May any merit gained by the production of this book go towards relieving the sufferings of all beings.

AND THANKS...

The two people who deserve most thanks are Julia Lewis and Subhadramati. Together we hatched the idea of the Anthology while sloping off for tea and cake with Srivati in Balquhidder Glen, Scotland, during a *Wolf at The Door* Writing Retreat. Both of them have been involved in the project from the start, and as my vision for the book expanded, both encouraged me to go forward, as well as supporting the project with immense practical help. All three of us chose the poems together. Julia Lewis put in many hours of administrative help with photocopying, and sending out e-mails and letters to contributors, as well as liaising with David Penn regarding book orders. She gave the benefit of her poetic experience and expertise in advising on various editorial matters and she gave advice on the final ordering of the poems. Subhadramati has assisted in giving timely encouragement, and ongoing support and advice on specific matters, particularly on budget, permissions, and distribution. Thanks also to Julia and Subhadramati, along with Subhadassi and Ananda, for carrying on a tradition of anthologies within the FWBO in the past. Grateful and loving thanks are also due to Ruchiraketu for technical support. Thanks to Varasahaya and Olga Kenyon for encouragement, and generous financial assistance. Thanks to Urthona (www.urthona.com) for assisting in contacting poets, and for raising the profile of Buddhism and the Arts worldwide. Thanks to Anne Berkeley. Thanks to Amarapuspa for sending out the initial flyers, and thanks to David Penn for holding the purse strings, and taking on the handling of book orders in the UK and Ireland. Thanks to Vimalasara (Valerie Mason-John aka Queenie) for encouraging me to think bigger. Thanks to Ananda and Manjusvara for *Wolf at the Door* (www.wolfatthedoor.org). Thanks to Padmakara for his design input, and Jen Brown for her origami. Thanks to Sarvapala for his accounting skills. Thanks to Ananda for his enthusiasm and design skills. And above all, thanks to Sangharakshita, who encouraged us to connect our writing with our Dharma practice, and without whom this book would not have happened.

Padmacandra, Editor

CONTENTS

Always More Apples

Into the Silence

THE YEARS

I have invited the years to join me
in this hut in the woods,
and the years have told me
I should love what happens —
this is the only world I can live in.
Nothing has been wasted, they say,
every featherweight of grief is precious.
The years have told me to be happy:
they say I should dance with joy
for my ordinary life.

Ian Tromp (Manjusura)

BORN INTO THIS WORLD

SOUL

We were beetles.
We were moths.
We were pine crickets.
We hurled ourselves blindly at any kind of firelight.
Then after dying we came back, were newly teething babes,
were waves tossing unsleeping all night long.
You and I in those days.

Ko Un
translated by Brother Anthony of Taizé and Young-Moo Kim.

BORN INTO THIS WORLD

Well, who, knowing beforehand,
would choose to be born
into such heat? But what if
that's exactly what we did?

We must have ignored the angry
red neon of the door sign,
smoke twisting out when someone
staggered, finished, toward home.

But there was a handsome man
tending bar, and a worried-
looking woman in a phone booth —
she was calling for someone.

We came to help, but quickly
forgot, and soon were like them —

weeping in a smoky tavern,
too drunk to put our feet on the floor.

Thomas R. Smith

MONTPELIER BOTANIC GARDENS

good morning

yes

   fine

good,   yes

I do

yeah

yeah,

advantageous

I think that's a good idea

uhuh

right

ahhh

uhuh

yes

grand

uhuh

splendid

right

that would be very good

yes,

I'd like that very much

uhuh

of course

that would give me a little feel for   uhuh

Yes

right

great

fine

sounds rather like fun to me

as well as serious fact finding

                                        business and pleasure
can always be combined
                        yeah
yeah
                yeah right
I'll not be chasing you
                you've given me a great deal to think about
        Absolutely
oh dear
                great   I'll do exactly that

    sounds like fun
                        been a long time   since

                    yeah of course

I'll hear from you
                        bye   (click)

Larry Butler
The poem 'Montpelier Botanic Gardens' was inspired by the voice of Gerry Loose.

A DRUNKARD

I've never been an individual entity.
Sixty trillion cells!
I'm a living collection
staggering zigzag along.
Sixty trillion cells! All drunk.

Ko Un
translated by Brother Anthony of Taizé and Young-Moo Kim.

THE HEART'S COUNTING KNOWS ONLY ONE

In Sung China,
two monks friends for sixty years
watched the geese pass.
Where are they going?,
one tested the other, who couldn't say.

That moment's silence continues.

No one will study their friendship
in the *koan*-books of insight.
No one will remember their names.

I think of them sometimes,
standing, perplexed by sadness,
goose-down sewn into their quilted autumn robes.

Almost swallowed by the vastness of the mountains,
but not yet.

As the barely audible
geese are not yet swallowed;
as even we, my love, will not entirely be lost.

Jane Hirshfield

PINE

The first night at the monastery,
a moth lit on my sleeve by firelight,
long after the first frost.

A short stick of incense burns
thirty minutes, fresh thread of pine
rising through the old pine of the hours.

Summer is trapped under the thin
glass on the brook, making
the sound of an emptying bottle.

Before the long silence,
the monks make a long soft rustling,
adjusting their robes.

The deer are safe now. Their tracks
are made of snow. The wind has dragged
its branches over their history.

Chase Twichell

TABULA RASA

It comes out of the sky
An orchestral flight
from the stars.

The geese I was watching
have blown the clouds apart.

Simon Millward

THE COLLECTOR OF JADE

In what existence could I be
this man, the collector of jade,
who can discourse so intimately
on saws and files, on routes of trade,
describe first-hand some nephrite mine
worked out by the Sung dynasty?

My grain's too coarse, yet I admire
the bamboo carved like an old pine
that holds his brushes, his seal-stone,
his scholar's coat's phoenix brocade,
the gnarled sculpture of uncarved wood
that warms his heart better than fire.

How I'd embarrass the great man
with hayseed Tao, a splashed excess
of pail-filler's philosophies!
All I could hope for, to be drawn
humping a load of firewood down
some pass, through mists and knotted trees.

Duncan Tweedale

THE WOMAN WHO LIVED IN A PEARL

Who knows when it started. First,
there were just suggestions of gauze

that thinned into the milk of opal.
Mornings mostly, as if it were always winter.

Not only the sky, that sphere of air
running rings around her: her skin turned

to almonds, a coating of sugar, coolness.
She'd slip her tongue around the idea of oyster,

track the snag of beard, a shell's camber,
and suck its sweetness. Until the blue hour fell

when the tang of sand flooded her mouth.
The taste of darkness at the heart of her.

Linda France

STRANGER IN SYDNEY GARDENS

A man is standing in the rain,
another tree, just standing in
whatever befalls. For me, walking
under my umbrella, he composes
the gardens as a sculpture might,
untitled figure, lifesize, beyond shelter
of the lush drenched canopies.

I take note of his thin hair,
town shoes and trousers, anorak
on which the rain has laid a yoke of shadow.
The air is lit by incense of strange candles
on that tree I think is the Tree of Heaven,
explaining itself now with sweetness,
and maybe he's arrested, beckoned

by vagrant perfume.
He's the look of someone just released

from his own story, and beginning
to remember the way the world
really is. I've a sense sometimes of
how little separates everything
from nothing, and all life exposed

to the glare of the stars.
There's a moment of amnesia on waking,
a free fall of the mind I feel now —
not who is he? but where am I? —
knowing only that anything can happen
and the heart wakes up: to the earthly kiss
of rain, these dazzling leaves.

Linda Saunders

PUZZLE

There is a long afternoon ahead.
You are laying out
the pieces of a puzzle —
edges on this side,
middles on that.

After a while
you begin to suspect
it's not just one,
but maybe three
different puzzles
bought from Oxfam,
jumbled in a bag.
Probably not all there.
And it seems like
some bits are never

going to fit.

'Perhaps it would be best',
you think,
'to throw away these ones.
They don't really go
with the others.
It will make more room
on the table.
I'll be able to see
what's what.'

And so you begin
throwing them away.
They get mixed up
with old apple cores,
used tissues,
and the screwed up
abandoned drafts of poems
in the copper waste paper bin
under the table.

The puzzle goes fine
all afternoon. And then
it gets towards evening.
Standing back,
you gradually begin to see
the gaps. And the lack
of pieces to fill them.

As you kneel down
and begin to delve about
in the copper waste paper bin
you can't help marvelling
that one small puzzle
could really fit in so much sky.

Jen Brown

CAMEO EIGHT

MIST AND A STAR IN MY ANTLERS.
I am here without paws.
A TRILLION BILLION SENSES
float on jealousy and envy.
Old age, ignorance,
and stumbling are a miracle.
INSPIRATION smiles like a boy
in a sand box shining
with mandalas
AND TWIGS.
Scattered among finger furrows.
A
SMOOTH
STONE
by a motorcycle
is perfect
as the clots
of wet green tea leaves
on an oak floor.

We guess that we
are streams in darkness.

Michael McClure

I LOVE AUGUST.

I love August.
I love the August sunlight.
I recall a billion years before.

Ah, my body grows wanton from the light of those ancient times.

Ko Un translated by Brother Anthony of Taizé and Young-Moo Kim.

MR PHEASANT

A pheasant
standing next to a dirt track
is surprised by the red rush
of a post van.
Annoyed,
he leans back,
utters a shrill, bad-tempered cry
and flaps his wings
indignantly.

Five minutes later
he's still there
looking distractedly about
as if thinking
I've completely forgotten what I was doing now!

Maitreyabandhu

A WORM THAT USED TO PLAY WITH ME

A worm that used to play with me
as a child told me:
No matter who calls,
don't answer yes too quickly.
They're most likely not calling you.

Ko Un translated by Brother Anthony of Taizé and Young-Moo Kim.

GLIMPSE

It was as if a window suddenly blew open
and the sky outside the mind came flooding in.
My childhood shriveled to a close,

thread of smoke that rose
and touched a cloud — or the cloud's

replica adrift on the slow river of thinking —
and disappeared inside it. In that dark water,
a new lily was opening, sky-white out of the muck.

It was only a glimpse, quick,
like a bird ruffling,

but I saw the flower's
beautiful stark shape, an artichoke
brightened from within by the moon.

A path lay shadowy under my feet,
and I followed it.

Chase Twichell

HORIZONS

SITUATION REPORT
for Padmakara

The path leads to a vast plain, and then ends,
petering into the expanse of grass.
We are lonely as stars out here. Sometimes
I remember the road through the forest,
its smells and colours and the beating drums,
but I don't wish for that kind of travel,
with its prophecies and wonders. Out here,
where to be lost means to be found, and home
is loss woven into a small thatched roof,
there is no anxiety of direction.
What can I say? I bake my own bread,
then sit at the centre of the turning world,
eating what my hands have shaped. The rains come,
but there is no place to hide, and no point
in dreaming of an elsewhere. The rains go.
I've a lover calls me over sometimes.
She softens the blow, the way night falls
as cold as a broken promise, out here.
You ask about a plan, about moving on.
I tell you: here, where the horizons
suffer neither fools' nor angels' pretences,
but melt the eyes' grip, and whisper only
grieving, it is best to learn to stay still.
And then, in the rigid bowl of the world,
every tree soft-stirring at the midday,
every blade of grass rich in its own light,
every weasel hunting, every mouse
and mouse-shadow crisp-drawn in the moonlight,
remind us that the path, not a path, just
a longing, leads only inward, to here.

Thomas Jones (Dhivan)

HORIZONS

They called it *white horizon:*
The bone between land and sky.
They called it *sad-shaped sleeping cloud:*
The light gone from the eye.

They called it *way untouchable:*
Distance beyond the skin.
They called it *far invisible kiss*
(From ancestors over the rim).

They called it *future water grave:*
A place for the ship from the shore.
They called it *dream impossible:*
There is *this* and nothing more.

They called it *silver magnet:*
The land of the Polar Sun.
They called it *crazy woman ridge*
(From the cliff she had overrun).

They called it *unknown love affair:*
The line between scarlet lips.
They called it *happy latitude:*
The dance from the heart to the hips.

They called it *black ash walkway:*
The space between earth and air,
They called it *hunter's shadowland:*
The place of the wolf and the bear.

They called it *place where words are born:*
The ledge where the snow owl winks.
They called it *secret waterhole*
(Where the singer sits and thinks).

They called it *come up here to me*
And *I will come to you.*
They called it *crimson angel-grace,*
When wings were breaking through.

Padmakara (Roger Bygott)

MAITREYI AND THE OWL

I'd set my shrine up under the window-ledge.
On it: the Diamond Thunderbolt Buddha
and three white candles in burnished holders.
I'd sit there late in meditation
candlelight hollowing my sitting-room cave,
the wind abroad on the hills, and two or three
times an hour, a miniature artillery
of raindrops in handfuls against the pane.

Dawn and dusk melted away without incident;
it was on the fifth or sixth night that it happened.
The weight of my body had fallen away
from its bones outwards and downwards; the breath-thread
so fine that the lungs, like tents of silk
on a windless day, hardly shimmered around it.
From this depth of quiet, as half the round world
slept and sped through enveloping darkness

came a sudden half crack, half thud on the window.
My body was jolted wide-eyed before
my mind could catch up, and it saw the owl
recovering, staggering upwards and backwards,
the work of the shoulder-wings finding the real space
was not there in front where the candles were burning,
the bird righting itself from the stun, until

it could swerve away with my thoughts alongside it.

Next morning a pale mist hung over the valley;
a pale sun behind it. All was as I had left it
except that the daylight revealed on the window
a trace of the bird's collision: two arcs
where the oil from the wing-feathers pressed it and, lower,
the triangular mark of the head — a dovelike
bow with incipient arrow pointing
directly over the unreachable Buddha.

Julia Lewis

GHAZAL (BUDDHA)

Even if we can't see it,
we bow down in our own perfection.

The world is this mirror: our constant
re-telling of the image before us.

Time only serves the lament of the world.
There can be no shadow without the lust for shadow.

Fire placed on the highest ground. A golden thread
of sympathy connecting us through all darkness.

Surely this is reason enough to smile?
Trust in our goal; let things happen as they should.

David Keefe (Manjusvara)

HIMALAYAN RAIN

We'd caught the bus from Kathmandu, to trek
the Everest trail. Up and down, against
the grain of the mountains, we walked until
our shaking legs steadied. The days were full
of wooded ridges and swaying bridges;
I'd never been so far from modern life.
One rainy day we detoured off the main
trail to visit a new-built cheese factory;
stock fences and alpine trees contrasted
with the huts and chickens of village life.
We drank tea in a dark wooden kitchen;
I went out on my own to look around.
A sound like goat-bells pulled me round a barn:
drips drumming on the metal lids of churns
lined up under a gutterless roof-eave.
The splash-notes of the shining drops left half-
imagined melodies hanging in mist,
took me through its living curtain of beads
to where music heals what time exiles: cloud-wrapped
among the vastest invisible hills,
I was played to by rain on silver chimes.
How I loved that illusion of heaven;
I heard; I was a believer. Years on,
last winter, at the back of a Welsh barn,
a line of icicles along a low
roof-edge rang at my touch just like those churns.
But I would have needed a hundred hands,
a mind as subtle as the rain, to make
that music, go through the curtain again.

Thomas Jones (Dhivan)

ARRIVE IN DEHRADUN

At the side of the road
a barber's chair —
the mirror hangs from a fence.

Jayne Wilding

BEYOND THE VILLAGE

Arrive at the nunnery,
the sound of bees —
nuns praying.

Jayne Wilding

SO GREY

so grey
     the boat
seems to float
     in the sky

so tiny
     the people
seem like ants —
I could eat them

Larry Butler

AT SARNATH

The stones from the Dharmarajika stupa
have been taken away
to build a market in Varanasi;
only a circle on the ground
marks the place where it stood.

You may wonder if it matters
that old stones move
to build a market in Varanasi,
although they drew the sky down
for centuries and sang like pilgrims.

The stones from the Dharmarajika stupa
were carted away
to build a market in Varanasi.
You may wonder
does it *matter* if old stones move?

Although they drew the sky down
and sang for centuries,
there's only a circle on the ground
to mark the site for pilgrims.

Varasahaya

SEQUENCE IN A STRANGE LAND

I.

Rusty pine-needles
Sprinkling the green-mossed top
Of an old boulder.

34

Spring buds,
Half-opened, shiver
In untimely snow.

Two or three buds
Are enough to show that Spring is here.
A few words
Are sufficient to say what the heart means.

I do not care at all
About writing any more poems.
Enough if I can say
How the heart bleeds and bleeds.

White wings flash, then nothing
But blue sky.

A long road,
An empty house,
And at the crossroads
Someone watching,
Someone waiting.

Mandalas
Need
Space.

A gift of violets
For the Buddha
And me!

In the front garden
Red tulips, yellow daffodils,
Stand tiptoe in sunshine
As it falls on the white
Walls where the green blinds

Have not yet been drawn.

Reading
Is not a Muse.

II.

Green pine-trees, and in between
The white box-like shape
Of apartment houses.

The sun sets
Behind dark woods.
Clear voices carry
Over mirror-like water.

Past the eaves of the sauna
Swallows, newly arrived,
Darting, swerving.

Somehow, today
I think of the blue poppy
That grows in the Himalaya.

Sangharakshita

HAIKU

Thrown on the white wall
Shadows of flowers
Have nothing to say.

Sangharakshita

SURFACE COUPLETS

From the bottom of the sea
The surface seems deep.

Haiku are only superficial
To the extent you are not drowning.

This is why the enlightened
Get bypassed in the street.

The astronomer comes back
To the beauty of the moon.

Padmakara (Roger Bygott)

WEIGHTLESS, LIKE A RIVER

I heard of a teacher and went to meet him.
In the monastery I studied his words
and the way he moved his body.

He seemed weightless, like a river,
both in his words and in his body.

Dawn zazen, the windows'
river light... I heard
his bare feet on the wood floor.

All the slow fish of ignorance
turned toward the sound.

Chase Twichell

THE CALL OF THE FOREST

TREE

It is foolish
to let a young redwood
grow next to a house.

Even in this
one lifetime,
you will have to choose.

That great calm being,
this clutter of soup pots and books —

Already the first branch-tips brush at the window.
Softly, calmly, immensity taps at your life.

Jane Hirshfield

NOTHING REMARKABLE HAPPENS

Away from the furnace
In this greenish gloom
In this dusty coolness
In this quiet exhaustion
Beneath the panting holly oaks;

Only the little adventures
Of numberless small legs
As they rummage and rustle
Through the shrivelled layers.

Even when Hannibal came this way
They noticed only a deepening shade

From the tender spread
Of an elephant foot,

And some while later
The precisely placed hoof
Of a Moorish pony.

Dhruvasimha

THE CALL OF THE FOREST

What does the forest whisper
With every wind-stirred leaf,
From many-centuried oak tree
To hour-old blossom-sheaf?
What does the forest whisper
When nightingales are dumb
And cicadas fall silent?
The forest whispers, 'Come'.

What does the forest whisper
In sunshine and in shade,
Down every moss-hung alley,
In each deer-haunted glade?
What does the forest whisper
When full or crescent moon
Steeps nodding crests in silver?
The forest whispers, 'Soon'.

What does the forest whisper
From depths primeval, where
A sound is lost in stillness
As clouds dissolve in air?
What does the forest whisper

When from the darkling bough
Drop one by one the dead leaves?
The forest whispers, 'Now'.

But the whisper's a dream-whisper,
For years on years have flown
Since oak and ash and holly
Could call the land their own.
The whisper's a dream-whisper,
For Cities of the Plain
Usurp the once-green kingdom
Of forests they have slain.

The whisper's a dream-whisper,
For 'forest' is a dream
Of days when Man through Nature
Had sense of a Supreme.
The whisper's a dream-whisper
Of a time when he could feel
In the pressure of the actual
The touch of the Ideal.

The whisper's a dream-whisper,
But dreams are of the Soul
And Soul itself a forest
Beyond the mind's control.
The whisper's a Soul-whisper,
That like a muffled drum
Calls, 'From your mind-built Cities,
O Man, to Freedom come!'

Sangharakshita

THE SPOILS

After the forage, dark comes on,
the carpet's covered with newspaper spread
    with the spoils of the soil, all shapes
and colours, mis-shapes, ambiguous colours,
    fungi waiting to be labelled.
One has a mauve subtler than reflection
    of cloud in water, another
a delicate cream skinning to crimson
    behind gnaws and bruises, with moss,
needles, torn leaf at the root. A spectrum
    of earth-smells; ripe, soapy, gluey,
peppery, putrescent; and the textures
    that go with them, from silk to slime,
rasp and flake, powder or deliquescence.
    Each wears its history; the mark
of insect-eggs, loose spider-threads, or where
    a twig caught on its way to mulch.
Some I appease with names from the field-guide's
    fashion-plates. Others, though, don't match
anything exactly; either the gills
    don't buttress rightly with the stem,
or the spore-print looks wrong. Born days ago,
    some still with fragments of the caul
that wrapped them, they seem older than the house,
    as if they'd sucked in through the web
of mycelial threads all the memories
    of the parent wood; storms, burnings,
night-cries. And as the streetlamp flares to red
    I hold on to the dusk, needing
the contemplation that, immediate
    as mist or woodsmoke, surrounds them.

Duncan Tweedale

TREES : A SEASONAL SEQUENCE

I

Red. For example the cherry
 prunus avium
in a patch of civic ground or suburban front garden; part of the
 blossom festival,
dawdling through passably anonymous summers. Whose
 gossipy leaves
will quieten in autumn, limp elliptical firedrops
 that hang
on a vertical axis (without wind, as though weighted). Its branches
 extend
to curve up like loop-fringed arms on a long sung note. If a breeze
 should disconnect
a leaf it seems arbitrary — they'll all go together when the tree thinks
 now
as though hold and relax of the hold were
 an act
of musculature. In fact, leaves are shrugged off with
 corklike callouses,
cell-barricades at the leafstalk. Hundreds of mouthlets
 gape red, slacken;
daunted, as though before railings, by lack of admission.
 Abscission. Sap
gated; each leaf placed outside the enclosure. Cold
 turns the keys.
The whole Order of winter trees resumes fasting
 and abstinence.

II

Silver. Thick-muscled, fissured roots
like limbs, almost level
with human eyes, of heaved-up
or sinking elephants

plunged knuckle-, knee-,
or shoulder-deep in a steep
English daffodil bank.
Old beeches; watchers

of a square stone house
with rained-on eaves
warmed from within
by light.

A traveller's horseshoes
might slow here, for
it is February, the daffodils
not yet out in the verges

to strike spring fire
from the hooves,
and February's purpose
uncertain as rain-light.

Indoors, perhaps steam
and a child sat reading
as rain-troop rattles
attack and recede

over the gutters' quiet
glops and gloops.
Meanwhile these watchmen
never challenge.

They let and are let to be;
majesty evoking majesty.
Their sodden skin,
in places shrunk, in others

sagging, a mark of what
is available, neutral,

to one who stands guard,
skeleton by the gate.

To greet them
with outstretched arm
and palm cupped
brotherly, reassuring,

around their humped watchfulness —
at the same time to watch, yourself,
how they dry their vast crowns
under hanging skies

you may feel the fine rain
fall the length
of the funnel
of your upturned nostrils.

III

Green. Nature's verticality

   having sped from seed
   balanced itself with a few side-strokes —

become nature's sketch

   — though not spared the bureaucracy of forming needles.

***

The monotony,

the extreme standing-up,
of the log road to heaven.
Ants form a dual carriageway.

***

Lower rungs

(within reach of goblin fingers)
clogged; their long pale dishcloths

belong to the kingdom of roots.

***

Larchbone of my spine!

an arrowhead loosed toward puberty
    bearing a mouth that gasped 'Wait!'

        to the zinging wind & piles of unwashed dishes.

***

Larch fronds. Oh, new

spring green on timeless summer blue,
to lie horizontal under your spars

& learn to swim the sky with you,
paddling the emptied pink gloves of my palms

    ***

until the stars glitter on the draining-board of the dark.

Julia Lewis

HOW AM I DOING?

Another day opens to the same ripping, petulant wind
as it opened to yesterday
and the one before.
I to my station
blanketed and wrapped
like an old lady frightened of the cold
or on her knees to Jesus.
I sit
whilst the wind throws dead wood at my tin roof
or tries — in vain — to break the spine of a neighbouring tree.
A brass band, heavy on the trombones, thumps again and again
through the same few bars.
Occasionally, my heart yelps
then I soften my eyes
and let my throat become so soft
that it could be cut in two by one sharp knife.
Wishing to postpone,
I try, by unclamping my narrowed shoulders
to find... peace, I suppose, or love.
How am I doing?

Maitreyabandhu

MEDITATION WITH BIRCH TREE, NOVEMBER

The stripped tree, scraffiti of branches
against morning's dull steel beyond
the window. When I close my eyes
it seems lighter inside, as if I'd hoarded
summer and my skin shone inwards.

Snipped threads of birdsong stitch me
to the nakedness of everything, twigs
and invisible stars, lives subliminal
as the purr of buses climbing the hill,
my breath breaking along a shore.

I'm awash with a scum of thought,
flotsam of plans, stillness, change,
till I open my eyes and find it's all
changed into itself: the birch tree's bark
exactly figured in the same silver as the sky.

A last gold leaf hangs like a coin
at just that point where in June
light pierced through tenements of leaves,
birch and dark pine lapped so thickly
as to afford just one keyhole to the eye.

Linda Saunders

MIDWINTER BIRCH TREE

Look again and the world
is always more exact, bolder
or subtler, than remembered.
The birch tree now

and black turrets of yew rocking behind
the flat roofs of garages proofed
with some metallic membrane
that spreads rain-slick like a sheet

to rescue the falling light.
Bare branches of the birch jig and flail

as the wind wrestles their knowledge
of stillness (in the roots' fastness),

their poise in the air.
And only yesterday even the furthest
twiggy capillaries, flexed or pendant,
were so still

that each carried its own mane
of snow crystals — impossible,
yet the mist's frozen breath
held them there.

Linda Saunders

TEA MIND

Even as a child I could
induce it at will.
I'd go to where the big rocks

stayed cold in the woods all summer,
and tea mind would come to me

like water over stones, pool to pool,
and in that way I taught myself to think.
Green teas are my favorites, especially

the basket-fired Japanese ones
that smell of baled hay.

Thank you, makers of this tea.
Because of you my mind is still tonight,
transparent, a leaf in air.

Now it rides a subtle current.
Now it can finally disappear.

Chase Twichell

RAIN IN IVY

I'm pondering the question
What hunts the leaf? No answer.
In the Monastery kitchen,
a dozen of us work in silence.
A koan is a monastery in your own head,
said Ta-hui, and as I set out to peel
a crate of acorn squash, I think he's right.
Rain makes the ivy move, as if
it were actively climbing.
It's metaphor to which my mind clings,
always too busy to see its own true nature.
I sharpen the knives just as my father
taught me, except here you don't spit
to wet the stone. I found the pocket knife
he lost, and hid it. I still have it.
I'm wondering where it is,
so when the drum sounds
marking the end of work time
I still don't know what hunts the leaf.

Chase Twichell

THE GOOSE AND THE BOTTLE

There is a goose inside a bottle.
There is a bottle with a goose inside.
How does the goose get out of the bottle?
How does the goose stay alive?
How does the bottle stay unbroken?
Where is the goose? Where is the bottle?
You are the goose. You are the bottle.
You are the goose inside the bottle.
Close your eyes: the goose is inside the bottle.
Say it: the goose is out of the bottle.
Believe it: the bottle is not broken, the goose alive.
Open your eyes: the goose is out of the bottle.
There is the goose. There is the bottle.
You have become the goose out of the bottle.
You are not broken. You are alive.

Linda France

TOMB OF TOOLS

TOMB OF TOOLS

The sea flooded the salt ponds on the Mankyŏng River
and Su-kil *ajosshi*,
who used to play the drum so well,
who had gone out to gather salt
in the midst of that maelstrom,
was swept away in the flood.
They never found so much as a shoe,
let alone his corpse.
Su-kil *ajosshi's* brothers
and his married sisters
debated
and decided to build him a cenotaph
in which they laid
the tools Su-kil *ajosshi* had used:
hoe, mattock, spade, and rake,
with the handles removed.
So he was buried in the ancestral cemetery.
A tomb of tools it was.
For some reason the village kids never went near that tomb.
For some reason that false tomb was frightening.
But three years later,
lo and behold, Su-kil *ajosshi* came back, alive.
His brothers at first recoiled in horror,
thinking it was a ghost.
It was only when Su-kil had shouted out several times:
I'm not a ghost, I'm not,
that they embraced him
and wept, exclaiming: *It's a dream, he's alive!*
Swept away in the flood,
swept far out to sea,
he came across a plank,
a narrow escape if ever there was,
and was swept down to the sea off Ch'ilsan

where he came across a boat
and the sailors declared:
In return for saving your life, you must serve us for a bit.
For the next three years he cooked the meals in the boat.
At last he escaped at Popsang-p'o and came home alive.
Su-kil *ajosshi* dug up the tomb,
retrieved his tools,
fitted them out with new handles,
stuck one into the ground and said:
You're alive, and I'm alive,
there's a lot of work to be done, as ever.

Ko Un
translated by Brother Anthony of Taizé, Young-Moo Kim and Gary G. Gach.

DREAM OF THE SINGING GRAVEYARD

Marble headstones. Flatstones.
White; yolk-delicate veined.
Deep-fluted bellied urns

and smooth cool pages.
Spaced, wealthy, silenced.
Only necklace ivy, spiralling

round slab and column,
stirred: a webfoot creature
unitracking upwards, slight

against the mass, live
against th'unlive, lithe
against th'unbending.

Most green, it seemed,

to all that white. And then.
Those buried treasure-chests,

their lungs their larynxes
their pharynxes, because
they could they did —

they sighed. A vocalise,
a hum, allowed new breath
old alleyways. From ground,

from grave, neighbour to
neighbour rumbled, spread
the modal exhalations

from the mouldering
dead. And then. No.
And *when*. The swell had

thickened, risen, purpling
the air, it curdled pure
harmonics, pleating chords

in sweetening clusters over
cherub stare and bleached
straw daffodil, until

the rediscovered plaintives
conjured one invisible,
indivisible choir

from call and answer,
restlessness and requiem. None
survived the breaking waters.

Julia Lewis

FIVE LESSONS

Burn your books:
All will be learnt
From your empty shelves.

Throw out your lover:
All will be learnt
From your empty bed.

Tear down your house:
All will be learnt
From your poor foundations.

Discard your clothes:
All will be learnt
From your nakedness.

Let go of your body:
All will be learnt
From your epitaph.

Padmakara (Roger Bygott)

THE YEAR I GOT RID OF EVERYTHING

A huge invisible magnet dragged me
up into its powers. It lifted me high above
the beautiful wool carpets and the books.

I put on a dress made of bones
and danced alone in the great emptiness.

Chase Twichell

TO EKAZATI

A Tibetan protecting deity

Lady with one plait, one eye, one tooth,
Dancing implacable on the glittering palace
Of bones which is this world where we shall all
Die, and most have died already, love
Of my life, I offer you this skullful of blood
Which is a poem spilled out on the page.
Suck out the marrow from my bones, drum
On my distended skin, unpick my sinews
And tune them for your lute-strings. All of me
Is gone already but that ball of fire,
My heart, lost in the burning sea that time
And passion fling around us like napalm
Or permafrost. Lover, mother, protector,
Guiding me in the maze of seven circles,
Embrace me. I shall know you in the dark.

Grevel Lindop

DAKINI OVER NEW YORK

When I found the email was from Martha Vine
— tech' manager for some digital recording site —
I was surprised to find, alongside facts about lasers
and lead-in times, a recipe for yam and cinnamon bagels.

And though my life is often like a subway train
that morning I was free, so after T'ai Chi I threw
together the dough, left it to rise by the east window
(Manhattan in full swing below), plumped my cushions,
lit a stick of incense — Indian, powder of a thousand
flower blossoms — and entered meditation.

She was garlanded with skulls and the sky's acetylene,
in her left hand the Statue of Liberty, in her right a flaying knife.
I was just accustoming myself to her breasts
— the way her nipples made flaming circles as she swayed
above the tower blocks — when she began:

firstly a cut round the thick of my thighs like a garter;
two others to girdle my neck and belly so true they were painless.
She stripped me back to something out of Gray's Anatomy,
a dance of death full of her mix of bliss and emptiness.

Risen, I shaped the bagels, watched each one swim to the surface
of the boiling water then baked them in the oven.
All I can say is I saw things different: alive less to each zero
of soft bread flesh; more to the freedom which seeded it —
that hole in its middle. The light at the end of her tunnel.

Subhadassi

SITTING

If you sit Buddha dies mother dies.
Don't sit.
Don't stand.
All five oceans six continents
       even
that cinnamon tree in the bright moonlight
here and there are all a boiling cauldron
with nowhere to put your feet down.
What's to be done?

Ko Un
translated by Brother Anthony of Taizé and Young-Moo Kim.

AZALEAS

The heavens rule by whim more than they do by reasoning, more by compulsion than request. Take, for example, this azalea bush. Notice its complexity and charm, its radiance and its abundance. But notice also the general chaos of its form, the derangement of its arrangement. It is as if some god, in order to relieve his infinite boredom, had deigned to build a model railway connecting up all the stars and then in a childish frenzy had suddenly thrown the entire contraption towards us. It presently stands in the middle of the air and I, for one, cannot decide if I really want to receive it.

Sasanaratna

SORROW

Every morning at five I'm woken
by thuds and taps at the window.
I tune them out, tunnelling under
my white cotton dark.
      After a week
of early alarms, I get up
to find myself face to face
with a magpie, caught mid-peck,
trying to steal the silver;

the glint of candlestick and chimes
all it takes to fire his desire,
deny the fact of glass.
      I cover
the shine with a cloth as if
it were a sleeping bird, close
the curtains and return to bed,

unable to settle for thinking about
all the things I've ever wanted.

Linda France

JOY

From an upstairs window, black-and-white
illuminates all the green, juicy with summer rain:

two magpies loiter, wing to wing, at the lip
of the pond; dip big bills into its dark bowl.

A patina of cobalt flashes behind bellies, fat
and soft as cream. There is chattering

and nodding. Later, through the gate,
over the glade of cottongrass, they're still

together, slicing the sky in two; spelling
it out — inky feathers, skin and bone.

Linda France

UNSATISFACTORY

So many years he'd wanted to know the word,
if there were such a word,
for the shine of the moon on the water.
Tonight, he found it.
Moonglade.
It wasn't anywhere near good enough.

He watched the others with their cookies.
Chocolate chip.
He watched their smiles and their teeth.
But he remembered his vow, and took an apple.
The apple appeared shiny, crisp, crunchy.
Outside, on the path to the shrine room, he took a big bite.
Mush.

He bowed to the Buddha.
He recited the refuges and precepts.
Unsatisfactory.
But better.

Tony Press (Acarasiddhi)

INCANTATION

Three times roon I wauk the puil
Tinklin watter. Puddock sweel

Inno memory's fykey pyoke
Stap the image, tie the knot.

Syne, fin hyne awa I gyang
Inbye aa thon sichts are thrang

Fa'd hae thocht that Loch an knowe
Cud set the senses in a lowe?

Three times roon I wauk the puil
Sun an meen an puddock sweel

Lest thon ferlies I should tyne
Cherm an chant shall mak them mine

Sheena Blackhall

GETTING THROUGH THE WAKING HOURS

Schopenhauer's advice
was to consume a toad
first thing in the morning
so that one wouldn't encounter
anything more disgusting
during the course of the day.

Portraits of this philosopher
emphasise his great rock of a forehead,
the wild grass of his hair
thinned down, having been torn out
by decades of dissatisfaction.

As a poet, I would prefer
to be remembered for my ears
and how listening saved me
from the heaviness of thought,
how words just came to me
in the middle of the night,
like birds that couldn't stop singing.

My advice would be
to learn to adore the stillness,
to want to fill oneself with it.
Then the secret world will respond,
just as it is. It will run down the mountainside
looking for you.

Rachael Boast

BLESSINGS

May your smile melt your ice-cream.
May you laugh when you put your foot in it.
May people fall over backwards for you.
May all your friends be followed by futons.
May your fridge always surprise you.
May all your accidents be works of art.
May your bathroom mirror giggle.

Padmakara (Roger Bygott)

A FRIEND

Hey! With the clay you dug out
I fashioned a Buddha.
It rained.
The Buddha turned back into clay.

Clear skies after rain are pointless.

Ko Un
translated by Brother Anthony of Taizé and Young-Moo Kim.

FOR A LIVING

(n) an article of furniture for sitting or reclining;

(v) to lie in ambush; to lay oneself down for rest or sleep;

(n) the den of an animal (such as an otter);

2:15 p.m. Jefferson High School

For some reason I mentioned a classroom I'd seen with two couches in it.

'Yeah, we should have a couch in the class, Mr. Press. That would be so cool!'

There are plusses and minuses to classroom couches. They can create cozy reading areas, something I really like, or they can be rewards for good behavior, or even a place for a quick teacher's catnap during a prep period. But, they can also create problems, as even fourteen year olds still climb and jump, and love to claim and scuffle over turf of any kind. Finally, couches can act as sirens, incessantly singing their sleep-inducing song to bored or sleep-deprived teens.

'I don't know. I can't say that I'm thrilled by the idea of a couch in here.'

'No, really, just think about it. It would be perfect against the back wall, too. In fact, if we all contributed five bucks, we could get a decent one! What do you think? And maybe an extra five bucks from each of us for your *retirement fund*, too, hint, hint.' Entire rows of students chimed in affirmatively.

'It's not the money, though that's an attractive offer, especially the bribery part, but I think we'll continue with the furniture we have.'

6:45 p.m. San Francisco

Walking to the Buddhist Center on a bitterly cold evening, I was startled to spot a large couch on the sidewalk ahead of me. A couch? Instantly, I thought of the classroom, and the giddy excitement in the room while we had briefly bandied the couch question. Who had a truck tonight, I wondered, or a big enough car, that could hold this couch? We might be able to snag this couch, assuming it was in decent shape, and bring it back to my school after Sangha Night. Wouldn't that be a treat for my 9th graders tomorrow! They'd love me, at least for a while.

I walked up to the couch, which was on its side, and which proved to be quite large. I looked closer, and it was in decent shape (for a sidewalk couch). I began to stretch my hand over the material, but as I did, I sensed a movement, and realized that underneath the couch, on the surface of the sidewalk, was cardboard, and upon the cardboard was a person. This couch, however it had come to be on the sidewalk of Bartlett Street, was shelter this night for someone. A large sheet of plastic, which I hadn't before noticed, had been rigged up to block out some of the night's chill.

I quickly detoured into the street, and then back onto the sidewalk on the other side of the couch/shelter. In fifteen seconds I was entering the center. In fifteen minutes I was meditating. In one hour the hard rain began. In three hours, as I hurried away down the sidewalk, the couch, person, and the hard rain remained.

Tony Press (Acarasiddhi)

AQUAE SULIS

Always somewhere there's a man
in a torn mac
going quietly downhill
with a bad cold, a slow puncture,

an out of date map
and 10p short of the train fare.
Always there's a thin man in a bar
who hasn't slept for two nights

and can't make out what town he's in
but when the time comes god damn it he'll
go down fighting.

And when the gloom is inhabited only
by the slack syntax of a laid-back cabbie
he weaves over to you and rasps
guess there's someplace this all makes sense
but sure as hell we ain't head'n' there.

Usually there's a badly-tuned radio
balanced on a window ledge
playing Dylan, or *let the good times roll,*
the words slugged senseless by traffic.

Towards dawn there's a clean half-moon
touching the spires
while a man dreaming in a distant room
cries out for more dishcloths.

And in Queens Square a down-and-out
gropes for pockets which always elude him
with fingers that will not feel
for a lighter that never worked anyway.

Stephen Parr (Ananda)

from HAN SHAN EVERYWHERE

Clarkston station missed the 6.30
half an hour to wait on a red bench
in the sun with coffee and chocolate
an apple and nothing to do. What
more could I want: less busy traffic
on Busby Road, more twitter of blackbirds,
a girl with big silver circle earrings
turns revealing 3 white stripes on her blue
track suit trouser? That's all I need.

Larry Butler

HAN SHAN STANDS ON MONDAY

Han Shan stands on Monday
in the unusually long post office queue
due to the temporary closure for refurbishment
of the Kelvinbridge branch. This was an opportunity
to wait and consider the possibility
of never losing time again, and putting aside all pretence
to achieve anything ever. He rested
eyes closed swaying like a tree. The queue went faster
than on other Mondays.

Larry Butler

ON THE TRAIN TO BASINGSTOKE

Opposite me, across the gangway, on the red-upholstered seats
sits a youngish man in a blue shirt. His feet are planted
squarely apart at the end of his navy blue trousers.
His blue tie has lilac and pale blue squares on it.
He wears small, metal-framed glasses.

On his knees he has a very slim lap-top computer and he talks
into a mobile telephone; about door details,
brush details — whether they can be glued to wooden doors because
they've always been routed-in before.
He is concerned about the white wall.

I wonder what he does on Sundays. There are creases
across the middle of his well-polished, black, leather shoes
like he crouches down a lot.
The inside pocket of his navy-blue jacket is frayed, showing
some white fabric. His brown hands now hold a pen firmly.

He is making decisive marks on the stapled sheets
resting on his diary. The pen is a propelling pencil.
He is called Matt. The train has stopped by a line of oak trees
with the sun shining on them. Another train whistles past.
A child laughs. Somewhere behind me a cellophane wrapper rustles.

Matt shuffles his papers. We are on the move again.
He is called Matt Saunders. The sun is hot.
The train slows to a station. A small row
of old fashioned shops. West Byfleet. Cantilevered
training desks — the client wants to fit cable trays underneath.

He's phoning to ask the price. They're 800 wide.
By the track, the leaves are dying from the edges inwards.
One has brown edges, then a part that's yellow,
before a perfectly green but shrinking centre.
We are miles down the track, stopped again, and again
there are oak trees.

Jen Brown

FOR A LIVING

What does it mean to succeed
in the world of work?

I think I'd better tell you,
as the lush countryside
flashes past the train window,
that I'm only writing this poem
so that the young woman
sitting opposite me
might consider whether or not
she ought to be
taking up three-quarters
of the table space

with her laptop, papers
and mobile 'phone.

I'm only writing this
to see whether or not
my Big Value Exercise Book
will get fair consideration.

Rachael Boast

TRANSACTION

Coming to buy eggs, you wear
the lacy hand-knit cardigan,
your camel-hair coat, good
shoes, a hat and orange lipstick.

Eighty-something and accustomed
to service, you stand waiting,
trusting the small unspoken
ritual that I will see.

I leave the till and come to help.
Choosing among the tray of eggs as carefully
as I would have chosen
for my own grandmother.

You expect no less of me.
Always, I ask how you are.
You reply evasively, politely
avoiding raw reality.

Praising your fortune,
you tell me about a brother

who drove a hundred miles
to see you, sick at Christmas.

Today, fresh back from visiting,
you say that you'll be leaving
and how you will miss people — me
and the lady at the bank who smiles.

Jen Brown

SHOPPING WITH THE BUDDHA

He seemed to enjoy the drive.
Not so much the view,
although I noticed him noticing the man
stood in the allotment
as we turned left towards Asda.
No, it was the breeze.
He leant his head out of the window
like a dog, closing his eyes sometimes
to inhale the world.

As I pulled into the parking space
and turned off the engine
he was already opening the door
and making for the trolleys.
A few people turned to stare,
but not many.
This is East London after all.
My surprise was that he didn't know
that he needed a pound coin.
I assume omniscience;
he assumed freedom and trust.

I let him push the trolley.
How could I have stopped him?

He had already refolded his robe across his shoulder
and was off into the vast cavern.
Knowing we needed vegetables,
another assumption:
that we would focus on our needs,
move mindfully, no energy (or money) wasted,
and be done in half an hour.

But no. The Buddha wanted to see everything.
We walked up and down every aisle
so that he could marvel
at the choice of breakfast cereals,
taste the free samples of cheese at the deli counter
and stand quietly by the banks of chilled flesh,
his bare shoulder goose-bumping
before he moved on.

For a while I lost him.
Then hearing a distant, deep laughter,
saw a flash of flying saffron
as he go-karted the trolley down the middle aisle
towards the shelves of eggs.
He stopped like a professional,
delighted to discover the button for bored children:
one press and a chicken crows like morning.
He pressed it three times.

I love the Buddha,
even when we reached the checkout
and discovered the expensive chocolate cake
he'd put in the trolley,
and knew that he had no money.

As we put the shopping bags into the boot of the car
I realised that we hadn't spoken once.
'Did you enjoy that?' I said.
'I enjoy everything', he replied.

Srivati

MOP

A mop bucket stands in the corner of the bathroom
It is plastic and green, has a red squeeze-place
and a cheerful blue handle.
The mop itself is pillar-box red.
It is fitted with a special pump-action device
for easy squibbing.
Someone has left a pair of yellow Marigolds,
the whole ensemble an unnecessary collection of primaries

It is a 'house work can be fun' descendant
of the armoured bucket
we used to have —
big and oval and made of silver-grey metal
so that when you carried it, leaning against its weight
— against a precipitous sloshing and reeling —
the handle always dug into your hand.
And it hit the ground hard.
And its massy head
was always wet.

Maitreyabandhu

FRIDAY NIGHT

The fish and chip man stands, arms folded, rocking
on his heels behind steam and his glittering vats.
'Don't ever marry, son. Take my advice:
don't ever get married.' He stares past my head
at the windows of his shop front, through which,
though they're pasty with droplets of grease, we see
the raincoats and folded umbrellas of passers-by.

We're waiting on my order. Cod and chips twice,
one with crackling (I've got my eye on it, the piles
of golden gravel in the warming-box), two saveloi
and chips, with lots of vinegar. I finger the dirty
pound note in my pocket. The man continues to gaze,
now at the floor, now at the window, not speaking at all,
slowly blinking as he tips backwards, forwards, heel
to toe. In the doorway behind him the plastic ribbons
of a curtain wander in a draft. The chip man's wife
is beautiful, I know. She serves here on her own
sometimes, in a red and white polka dot dress. 'No,
don't ever get married.' When the chips are ready
he shuffles them dry and rolls the whole order
in JOHNSON SPEAKS. 'That's six shillings sixpence,
please. Well, don't listen to me.' The door tinkles
behind me. The sun's going down. The newspaper's
hot in my hands. I run home.

David Penn

TRIAL AT A BUS STOP

Dear Miss Strand,
I believe they're your girls in the red
and black? I saw some earlier today,
assembled round the bus stop opposite
the Harvester on Beulah Hill. I thought
I ought to tell you what was going on.
It's been a windy day, and days
like this induce a sort of skittishness,
I know — and I was once a teenager...
The leaves, red-ochre, brown, were rolling
round like overflow from pirate treasure,
gold that had escaped and hoped to creep
unnoticed through the grass. The girls

were all absorbed in circling round
each other in a complicated spiral, like
a time-lapsed opening rose or galaxy
in miniature. And at the centre
was a tiny girl, a black girl with
a red beret, round spectacles
and dimples that made mischief
round a gad-toothed smile. Her two front teeth
would loom like tigers' teeth and threaten
everything: the universe, herself included.
She was chubby, you might say, not fat,
full-cheeked, her hair in ribboned bunches
roaring from her head like smoke.

Whenever any bus drew up
you'd see the most extraordinary thing:
the girls would swarm around it like
a clan around a giant hog
and hammer on the doors. The buses, though,
are always full that time of day —
with other kids just out of school —
and so the drivers (God be with them)
wouldn't let them on. The girls
would fall back on themselves, a self-
enfolding wave, but this girl ran
at every bus and pressed some buttons
on the side that flung the doors
wide open — buttons that are only
for emergencies of course. You saw
the drivers cursing from their cabs,
but there was nothing they could do.
The girls all yelled when she came back
to them: 'Again! Again!', by this stage
having dropped all thought of getting
on a bus by any means. Each time
the doors slammed back it was as if
she'd opened up a wound in some

huge beast, or was provoking some
enormous dragon, playing round
its jaws. And these were double-deckers,
tall enough to scrape the trees.
They dwarfed us all like siege machines.

No other adult at the bus stop
did a thing, I have to say.
They fidgeted as if it wasn't happening,
checked watches, clouds, their feet.
I hardly knew myself what we
should do; I made a move as if
to stop the girls but felt more like
a stranded carp than anyone who could
command authority. I stood there,
brave in my imagination — folded arms,
expanded chest — but having no
effect: some village bobby of
the nineteen-fifties, stepping from
a time-machine to find himself
invisible. What shall we do?

David Penn

A WOMAN OBSERVED IN A PUB

The woman with the whipcord hair
does a bee dance from the loo.
She slow-zigzags across the floor,
uncertain of her step — as though
she's realised she's a tightrope walker
suddenly.

Foundation smeared like chalk,

black cherry lipstick, auburn hair;
her cheesecloth shirt, worn jeans
and satin bomber jacket
hang as loosely as a circus tent.
And at her table,
there's her boyfriend, holding court,
his gold-ringed fingers spread like
palace gates, his silvered glasses
too absorbed to point her way.
She sets down like a bird
and lights a cigarette, and stares at the wall
and talks towards it, nodding.

Like a puppet balanced by a leaden weight
inside her skull, she moves her cigarette
between her mouth and the space
in front of her, then leaves it
like a short white needle, dripping wraiths.
And as she leans
towards the invisible friend,
she holds a hand to him across the table,
and the boyfriend turns mid-tale
and freezes, watching.

The invisible guide is listening now,
and when he listens, he really listens
and when he speaks
he must be saying something good,
because she nods, and smokes,
and takes it all in.

David Penn

MEANING

is finally running out.
No matter how you plead,
this state of the art
opener will not mesh
with the Smedley's jumbo size
processed garden peas.

You grope tearfully for change
in a biscuit tin
brooding with blank moons;
carry the mush of cake
crumbs left from the funeral
as far as the bird table

then forget why.
I stand at the door encouraging
a terrified animal.
Try raising the left first,
then the right, I suggest.
Try taking a deep breath.

Now it's the turn of the new
minimalist quartz clock
on top of the TV.
What do all those
numbers mean? you ask,
Are they time?

Stephen Parr (Ananda)

DREAMING IS THE ONLY TRUE DEMOCRACY

A man stands under a tree in the rain.
He is watching a window high up in the building across the street, where
    a dancer is practising.
She moves in and out of view, making fleeting shapes, like brushstrokes
    in the square of yellow light.
Tonight she will dream of swans floating on a lake that reflects a grey sky
and he will walk in a desert, find a faded photograph and not recognise
    his own face.
In the silent room below, an old woman dozes by the fire,
orbiting the earth in a rusty satellite,
training her telescope through the
portholes on the turning world below.
At her feet a small ginger cat dreams of being a circus pony
while, in the kitchen, the electric toaster dreams he is an oracle,
scorching prophecies onto each slice as it pops up.
Outside the trees dream of honey and metal winds.
A car slides past in the night, scattering puddles into diamonds.
The child curled under a blanket on the backseat is adrift amongst a
    shoal of bright purple jellyfish,
and below the skin of the city the bedrock tumbles like rolling cloud.

Andrew Miller

BECAUSE

I behave this way because a voice in my ear instructs me in a meditation
    on the colours blue, green, mauve and yellow.
I behave this way because I am visualising them in the chakras above my
    head.
I behave this way because the Shaman, my teacher, is watching me
    through his visionary eye.

I behave this way because I must twirl on tiptoe and sing the colours on
    higher and higher notes.
I behave this way because he needs my help.
I behave this way because he believes I am a goddess and by eating a
    bowl of porridge I can demonstrate I am only human.
I behave this way because by walking in a figure of eight round these
    two trees I will earth my energy.
I walk very fast because there is so much energy coursing through me.
I behave this way because when I return the notes of his flute still linger
    round the walls of my flat.
I behave this way because if I prop the window open and create a
    thought path to him his spirit can escape.
I behave this way because he does not go and is floating in the sky of
    the carpet.
I behave this way because I can see pictures in the green glass of an
    empty wine bottle.
I am watching a Tibetan lama gracefully usher him out of a half open
    door.
But he keeps turning back.
I behave this way because every time I make the slightest movement it is
    magnified in his mind.
I behave this way because I must see green before I can move, blue
    before I can speak, and mauve before I can think.
I behave this way because I am waiting for him to phone me to prove I
    am not mad.
He does not phone.
I behave this way because the man who says he is a nurse is really one of
    my friends in disguise.
I behave this way because I must act out the story of being taken into
    hospital.
I behave this way because everyone here is in on the plot.
I behave this way because I must now repeat my thoughts and actions
    in reverse order.
I behave this way because at the right moment he will intervene and
    stop me sinking too far.
I behave this way because he keeps missing the right moment.
I behave this way because some destructive action is required and tearing

down this purple curtain over the door window is relatively harmless. I behave this way because they have put me in a blue room and injected me with something.

Pam Cooper

JUST IN CASE

Well yes dear, but you never can be too careful so just in case, take a hat and scarf. Just in case the weather changes over night. I don't want you catching your death if I'm late. And leave me your mobile number just in case I *am* going to be late. Mrs. Casey was stuck in Waverley for three hours last week, poor soul. And she has swollen thighs. No, she had swollen thighs before she got stuck at Waverley. She was attacked by hornets on a Quaker picnic, poor soul. And I'll give you my mobile number just in case you get stuck in traffic or something. In fact, best phone the station before you come out just in case they cancel the train. I tend to fear the worst, especially with *Virgin*. I like to leave nothing to chance, just in case. Especially with *Virgin*.

I'll see you at the station then, dear. Looking forward to it. Tomorrow. Four o'clock. Yes I know you know it's four o'clock. I knew you probably knew. ....Well, just in case you'd forgotten or jotted down the wrong time, dear. I've jotted down the wrong time on more than one occasion myself. And I'm very careful as you know. It's easily done. Oh and I've bought something for the twins. A fluffy rabbit and an Incredible Hulk. And I've kept the receipt just in case Deirdre doesn't like the fluffy rabbit. Well, because it looks surprisingly fierce for a rabbit. ....Sorry, I certainly *am* bringing an apple pie. I'm bringing one with a sort of wholemeal pastry just in case Lorna's still on that stupid diet. Well, because nobody should be that thin dear. It's unnatural. I'd get her tested just in case it's cancer..... No, I'm not being morbid. I'm being realistic.

I'll say goodbye now dear just in case my credit runs out. See you at the station. Tomorrow at four o'clock at the station then. Central not General remember. Yes, I know you probably did but just in case you'd got mixed up. Getting mixed up can happen to the best of us, dear. Oh, and just in case I can't make it tomorrow.... Well, you don't know what tomorrow will bring. Well there's this flu thing going around. Mrs. Casey was in an awful state, poor soul. Yes, she is rather unfortunate health wise. I took her round a flask of soup just in case she needed something hot. Anyway, just in case I inhaled her germs and succumb, or just in case I can't make it tomorrow for whatever reason, I sent that knitting pattern that Lorna wanted through the post.

.....Well I don't think I am, dear. That's a little hurtful. I prefer *careful* to *fussy*. The best laid schemes of mice and men gang aft a gley. This is from the mouth of our national bard, dear. And there's a lot of wisdom in those lines. It's certainly been my experience. I mean, it's a constant theme in literature. One of Thomas Hardy's characters pushed a vitally important note under the door and it went straight under the mat and was never received. Hardy really knew his onions. There were dreadful consequences, dear. Hardy knew about life. This chap should have double checked just in case. Sent two notes. Three. Phoned. So *often* things upset the best laid plans. Believe you me. You can't trust anything or anyone, believe you me. So you need to think of everything. You can never be too careful. Best to leave nothing to chance. Just in case.

Alastair Jessiman (Sarvananda)

ONE SMALL THING

If I had known all along
that that was all it was
I wouldn't have bothered to floss my teeth
or wear that stupid nylon tie
nervously purchased from *Top Man* on Princes Street.
(I never enjoyed the feeling of constriction at the neck
through which we project success).

Had I guessed

that beyond a thousand million worlds
(and each one full with millennia of the histories
of billions of citizens)
that One Small Thing was making its way,
faithfully,
to find me...

If anyone had remembered to tell me
how very trivial, this key, and light
at the exact moment when I was ready to listen,
I would have lain in bed longer this morning.

But as it is and as it stands,
I had to see it by and for myself
from the window of a car (of all places)
at the speed of a last straw, falling.

Bruce Peterkin

GENIUS LOCI

DOWNLAND RISING

Why should it be this place, not another,
the drooping mind drifts to? The high-hedged lane
rising from Itchen Abbas through the chalk
    to the secret grange, its long walls

capped and crumbling, cardiganed with ivy
and bitter nettles. There's blackthorn in bloom
and cowparsley's merciless elegance,
    and flints smoothed to divinities

whose names were lost long since. If one's shut out,
it's not from any richness, any depth
of joy or wholeness beyond the locked gate.
    A mower's there, a ball, a swing,

but nothing tempts dreams of a harpsichord
or gold-tooled morocco. It's just a glimpse
things might be otherwise. Of Sunday walks
    twenty years back towards freshness.

It's the eye greedy for a languid time
of myths and prospects. That wants to thread life
down the veins of a leaf, curve of a song,
    and, following, make them its own.

Duncan Tweedale

A DISTANT PROSPECT OF THE CITY OF WINCHESTER

1

All those eleven years he stood so close
words wouldn't gel. Out for a teatime stroll,

he'd be hemmed in by plots he couldn't grasp,

as if the saints of all those vanished churches,
St Alpha, St Oades, St Mary Kalender,
St Anastasius, held power there still.

Yards hid orchards, garages bowling-greens.
Turning a corner of wall, there'd be St Ruel
crouched with a brace of yellow hunting-dogs,

or Emma the king's mother, crossing the pit
of burning ploughshares to retrieve her honour.
In the cathedral, he'd make not for the diver

lifting foundations with his hands, but the grille
where Bishop Fox, ablaze in his cage of bone,
gapes at the arches copying him above.

2

Taking the town by surprise, tramping past reed-beds
through the horse-fields, he'd stop, become for a moment
some carter or packman from an old engraving,

who'd glimpse through trees the cathedral's great shed roof,
say, 'Nearly there', and plot for a change of luck.
But no gold paved the streets; the pubs were stocked

with the same drifters acting the same delusions,
floating six inches above the working week.
Turned out, they'd roam the water-meadows, dazed,

muddling through their stations of gall and wormwood
till darkness hid St Catherine's beech-wood cap.
Climbing the hill, he'd watch the layered cities

merge into anxious one. Best out of it,
among flowers like mantras — saw-wort, devils-bit —
free from ditches and bells, the duress of shadows.

Duncan Tweedale

from DEER RUNS

In cities, the runs are
mostly used by cats; are
lost in daylight under
the tramp of feet that pace daily
routines and routes
to and from places like
homes, shops and public libraries;
between which the humans make
automatic movements
— *walking to the grocer's* —
the mind elsewhere, a blur of
vague associations.

But late at night
you can get down low and smell them out,
and run them:
up this interesting dark alley,
across a grey puddle,
over this wall, drop into
a hidden office car park,
down these steps,
round some dead buildings, out
onto the street. Avoid cars.
Down the side of this closed restaurant,
through the half-abandoned grandeur
of Victorian civic life,

under a fire escape, over a locked gate,
onto a sudden expanse of once-cut grass,
rank with brambles, knotweed, nettles,
where hedgehogs prowl;
and onto this high, crumbling wall,
along the musty ivy, down
and — quiet here — a back garden,
may be a dog around; across the corner,
past a compost heap,
warm smell of clippings,
back onto the street, through
a stretched gap in a link fence
made by kids, who also seem to know
some of these runs,
across rails glinting in moonlight,
the oily, green-black gravel clinking,
humming wires overhead.
Then down a steep embankment,
littered with a sycamore, broken bottles, stones;
leap onto a pitted, empty footpath,
this dark corner smelling of piss,
back onto a lit street,

slow down, back on two legs,
slip into the yard door of the house,
make a mug of cocoa as if nothing had happened
for the landlord, who's watching TV.

Thomas Jones (Dhivan)

IN PERSPECTIVE

The sky behind this heath
is purple, then it is peacock blue, then
the kind of grey that can only be called slate

if the sheen of slate
is acknowledged.

Against it phosphorescent treetops mass
above less startling green. Below,
through meadow grass, glide
a jacket and a shirt,
nicely small.

Alison Clayburn

AS JOSQUIN WOULD

Not lines but arches, voices echoing
curve against curve, like ash-boughs interlaced
along the river. Swooping and gliding,
leaping with joy across a dust-lit space

where boxed kings moulder. Saints in gold and green
play hide and seek in their lime-washed recess.
And the arcs follow you out, over patched lawn,
to the closed factories with their broken glass,

acres of crinkled hangars in blank ruin,
where months ago the fork-lift trucks would scut
down aisles of pallets. Now there's a crude sign
hangs on barbed wire, 'No Larking About',

and you suddenly want to skip in the air,
to mock its negation with silly walks.
As Josquin would, who, faced with the despair
of years of conflict, fire or plagues' havoc,

would take a soldier's song or pop complaint
and build a mass out of a single phrase,
turning its commonness to sacrament.
As Hariprasad belies his bruiser's face,

heavy-lidded, raising the bamboo flute
to his thick lips, and with a half-smile frees
the spring that held him, to a chase of notes,
a float of breath, all light and entrances.

Duncan Tweedale

POET'S WHISTLE

My tin whistle's the kind the beggar plays
beside the Abbey doorway, his quick tunes
climbing the stone ladders with the headless
angels. I heard of a commuter who practised
his penny flute in traffic jams, light airs
weaving upwards out of the tedium
of engines, impatient horns at Blackfriars,
his skilful breath in time with solitude.

And sometimes I dream of a devotion
other than words, pressing my fingertips
carefully over the holes — if only
one pure note, a voice not cracked or squeaky...
Frère Jacques or a few bars of Greensleeves
are harder than you'd ever imagine.
Mostly my Feadog Original
Irish Whistle lies on my desk among
pencils and paperclips (where also
Manjushri wields his discriminating
sword, but holds the lotus in his left hand).

It reminds me of hours I might open
between the phone calls, deadlines, all that
business, and enter, its mouth to mine
in a kind of kiss — while I almost hear
the airs and reels still sleeping in its throat.

Linda Saunders

A POEM

This morning the garden wrote a poem
not about me although I was in it with
spring on dewy grass between my toes
and red blossom on a nameless bush.
The poem dug for worms then scribbled
on the neighbour's fence while white arms
opened & closed drawing long shadows
stretched across three gardens with paths
leading to middens by backgates
left open on Tuesdays when men come
to collect completed poems wrapped in
black plastic bags hidden in metal bins.
This morning I lost myself between words
distracted by a multitude of nameless birds.

Larry Butler

ON THE LAWN

What presses on my heart is greater life
like fingers on an antirrhinum's mouth
which isn't ready to open. I don't doubt

that life, like the lawn's daisy and eyebright
pressing on my feet, will find a way,
but it's not getting the angle right,
more like a thought-craft slicing a diamond ray
than the swallow's fast, low, fearless, dark flight
across the grass, or the toadstool's slow
self-unwinding into form. I lie flat
and press my face into the dense warm bed
of summer; I hand-stand and feel the taut
strength in singing limbs; then glimpse, upturned, red
geraniums' sheer blameless beauty on show.

Thomas Jones (Dhivan)

THE ALLURE OF THE LOCH

We are lured by the loch because the lull of its flow breaks the
monotony of the mountainside with an indolence deeper, even than our
own. That slow moving languor, nonetheless; that pure mass of
indifference, offers nothing really for the eye to hold and we soon feel
the ripples of dismay enclose upon us. We are saved from this solemnity
by the assertiveness of the oak; the confidence of the conifer; trees
which triumph over the waters of reverie. But we soon distrust their
stubborn authority. We soon become bored with the stillness. Then a
bird whose name we cannot recall traces in the air across the glen the
outline of an object which is not yet finished, not yet recognisable...but
which we will nevertheless one day find ourselves deeply desiring.

Everything we long for relieves the burden left by a previous image.
Every flower interrupts the language of another. And poetry heals with
the heat of a hesitant whisper, calming our thoughts by contradicting
the promise it made before.

Sasanaratna

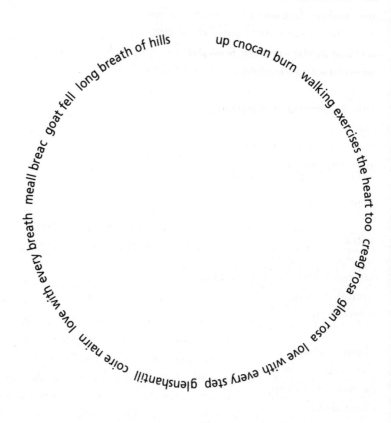

up cnocan burn walking exercises the heart too creag rosa glen rosa love with every step glenshantill coire nairn love with every breath meall breac goat fell long breath of hills

Larry Butler

PICTISH STONES

On the rocky beach at Badescaille
an old grey row-boat (stink
of voyage and rust)
and islands (water-
grey) and an old shoe

were among the ways that Scotland
opened itself to the mind's
eye, saying
make a sculpture or something
written, new
to this sandbeaten board —
stick something on it

(Elgin & Picardy:)

such as —
the pictures relieved
(say *eased*) from the stone at Elgin,
certainly shining
in brown rain,

a hunter, a hawk
and a couple of dogs —
the motion in them,
round about
of farmfields: redgold, greengold,
dark —
a shining net of economy

caught us
as the stone was made available to the wind's
eye, the crop

flattened
in silver swirl

and chalk-marks
fingered the stone to emphasize
the Double-disc and Z-rod,
Serpent and Z-rod,
Mirror

    *

The Picts (from the Latin *pictura*:
The Painted Ones? or The Ones Who Painted?)
refused to accept the invaders' alphabet
but dropped their lithograms here and there
to bond the fields together in various ways

they remain an enigma
the 14 basic symbols
bonded together in various ways

    *

her hand is pressed on mine
and populations come and go
economies fail

to arrange what there is to find
as the avenue lines the road
and turns, turns and again

her form on mine
and our hands as wide
as whatever comes to mind

Graham Hartill

ANIMAL CAUTION

Whenever I touch the cairn
marking the summit
of one of my parents,
touch the top stone,
an animal caution comes over me,
sinew and muscle like the brook's,
a sudden shivering
green-brown flame,
a ghost swimming
through me like a fear.
Soon they will be constellations,
and I a small tower of stones.

Chase Twichell

THE STYX FLOWS THROUGH BALQUHIDDER

Tapsalteerie doon the burn
The craikin craa an the turnin wirm
The smoodrach snaa an the tummelt cairn
Whummlin doon wi the lauchin bairn

Heelstergowdie ower the linn
Fur an feather an fang an fin
The faschious wife an the birsslin deil
The scholar priest an the eident cheil

Boats an biggins an grains o san
Fae Auchtermuchty tae Samarcand
Gae wallopin aff tae gweed kens far
Wi a soo, a doo an the Norlan star

Bible, compass are dinged tae nocht
The burn can neither be stopped nur bocht
Tho whyles it dwaums in a derksome puil
Up it gaithers wi breenge an sweel
Pitten an eyn tae clishmaclavers
Canty blethers an daft like havers.

Bide on the bank an ye can wave
As the hale jing bang lowps inno the grave
It winna be lang ye'll murn an greet
Thon ferlies thrang ye'll quickly meet
Twa blinks o an ee an yer life is ower
A nochtie wheech o stramash an stoor.

Sheena Blackhall

SUMMER RAIN

I woke past midnight
to the slightly burnt orange odor
of soft summer rain.

My wife slept beside me,
deep breath punctuated with
the little sighs of a dreamer.

Outside, pale moonlight
shone through the clouds, the great
evergreens dripping,

the katsura at the far end
of the garden turning
bright yellow already, although

it was early August.
I made a cup of tea and went

out to stand on the deck.

I've clung to this place
like Han Shan-tzu
clung to his cave near the temple

on his belovéd mountain.
I've watched these trees reclaim
a chunk of forest — slash,

waste and underbrush
when I came here
thirty long years ago.

No place is special
except we make it so
through myth or habitude.

The forest reclaims itself
as best it can. Can I
do less? 'No road leads the way',

Kotaro duly noted, his echo
of Han Shan an echo of Lao Tzu,
and hundreds of years between.

I love beyond words this quiet rain
in these trees, the rose
whose stark white blossom

lasts only a day, this garden
in moonlight, and the woman beyond it
who sighs, worried in her dreams

about her sleepless paramour
who rises in the night
to smell the rain.

Sam Hamill

GENIUS LOCI

Sometimes, as death came nearer, it seemed to him
that he would not mind becoming a *genius loci*,
a small protecting deity, for this place
of folded green, silver-grey rock, May blossom,
with its glimpses of stars, roots and mud.
It could be, after all, only a brief diversion:
in a few, or a few thousand or a few million
years it would be burned or covered with ice
or the planet itself, or the universe, would disintegrate
or otherwise unbe. In the meantime
he could tend it, discourage destruction, gently induce
such continuities of use, language, pathway, skill
as could be sustained. Nourish the dew, mitigate the intrusion.
And when all was gone, as it would be, he could keep
at least some tracery, some crystalline seed,
some impression or whorled print of what it had been
as nucleus or hint or inspiration
for another corner of some other world,
mental or physical or in-between.
Nothing could be kept, of course: it was all evanescent
as the apricot-lace buttress of the bunched and dissolving cloud
spilling now behind the oakwood and the white-rendered
barn above the red roadsign on the steep corner
where the fence was. None of it was either
physical or mental, it was all both and beyond both
but it was good and it was loved and there was something
founded within its lineaments that made it clear
how in its slow, elusive being or non-being
it returned the love and was also a kind of guardian
to those who noticed. And sometimes it seemed the noticing
was more important than both, and would go on.

Grevel Lindop

ALWAYS MORE APPLES

FLOWERS AND FRUITS

Two monologues from a still life by Fantin la Tour

We know we're only temporary,
that's clear from the knife
and the way we lie at the base
of this composition, on the table
and with the weapon projecting
between us. That knife will be raised
eventually, once he's done,
and when it is we're done for.

While we, uplifted by whiteness of our vase,
will not be consumed and,
even as we fade, we know that we'll exist
forever in the mind, not just of our maker
but of all the hungry people; hungry for our beauty
and hungry for their own.

Alison Clayburn

FRUIT

for Michael Hamburger

Let me list the apples that you gave me:
Berlepsch, after a German Count;
another, small, yellow-green, known as *Crispin* in England
but with a Japanese name, *Mutsu*, you'd find me later in a book;
and those, small, hard, crimson, with a taste some find too sour,
from the tree you'd grown from an apple
given you by Ted Hughes, from his garden;
there was *Belle de Boskoop*, Dutch in origin,
white, huge beyond known archetype to me,
hard, good for winter;
a Belgian, smaller, rather conical in shape;

still others: cousin of the English Cox;
and one identified by red stripes on a yellow ground.

No dream-work, but well-ripened fruit,
weight of a hundred hundred working-days,
so too the small but perfect yellow pear
hidden in the grass till deftly pocketed by you,
from the pear tree raised from seed.

Satyadaka

STILL LIFE

Chardin's silver goblet
Reflecting three apples
Into a spiral.

The glazed bowl
(With used spoon)
Fully emptied.

Two deep brown hazelnuts,
Polished and apart,
Rest on the folded ledge.

I ate quietly.
Dreams may decay,
But there are always more apples.

Padmakara (Roger Bygott)

INNOCENCE DRIVEN BY LION FACES
takes to its wings and listens with furred ears
to
WINTER
MORNING
LIGHT.
The stream warbles nearby
before sunrise.
My muscles swell when rain
moves through the grass shoots.
Remember gray sand
and propeller whirr
of wind-blown palmettos
and the apple that falls
from the truck and rolls
to
drop
through the sewer grating.

THIS IS A UNIVERSE
of
realms
that we swim through
while a horse neighs.

Michael McCLure

ASKING FOR RAIN

The Japanese Buddhist pilgrim Jojin, passing through the Chinese capital in 1073, became the first Master from Japan to be commanded by the Emperor to pray for rain...

I

I will begin under the crab-apple
in September — half-green, half-red
with the unripe and the ripening fruits
and the delicate twine of clematis;
the grass at its foot littered with the apple stunts,
rotting, and the wasps rising off them —
there is incense burning somewhere, there is mist
coming down from the hills to the Emperor's garden,
and I am afraid.

II

I will pray here for thirteen days,
all the birds pray with me:
their Spring menagerie vie-and-echo calling.
I will learn their faculty for talking
to the clouds, for telling what will happen
with the weather and the chances for rain.

Their swapping blossom-tales I envy,
their presences in trees — between seasons
of the living and the dead — are alive
to something, in some way I know nothing of.
No, not nothing: I have my glimmers,
glimpses of what they might mean —
and when I see them, I will write them down.

III

This tent is full of mysteries.
I lie awake and listen to the wind
and wonder if the rain will come tonight,
and whether it will stay long enough
for the Emperor to be pleased with my efforts
which he cannot govern, but
which I cannot possess alone;
he knows this, and I choose to be here.

Our conversations are all silence,
a history of listening from respective places;
his palaces are full of voices.
But sometimes when the wind drops
we can discern each other,
attending and immeasurably divine,
each in his own, and I know
he will permit himself a smile
in my direction.

IV

In the whole of the wet world
there is nothing like this mist
that sways over everything
so everything is seen —
the trees, the hut, the gardener's plot —
as if new-formed by looking,
the eye itself having found
its true object, learned its nature
in the nature of other things.

The body of the world breathes
and is saturated, laden with an air
that can change the shape of birdsong
and the calls of early risers

that float and twist and vanish
over the valley; its scent,
inborn and rich and palpable,
condensing over warm cheeks,
reaching the heart everywhere.

In the palace the Empress awakes
and seeks her favourite slippers,
faded beyond their value in embroidery;
slips on her gown and out
onto the balcony to let the air
wash over her, lip to thigh,
longing — only later — for the sun;
but I should not dwell with her:
the Emperor stirs by his favourite wife,

My master now, dreaming always of the rain.

V

Mistress, I use the lotus flower
      to make the rain,
a billion petals descending
to scent the driest parts of your kingdom:

    Lobelia
    Honeysuckle
    Coltsfoot
    Ladysmock
    Ladyslipper

and the ivies growing over the palace walls at dusk.

The lupins hold my secret in their bells,
bees turn silver in the rain pools:
and if you would only drink the drops that run

down the stems — let your lips drown! —
you too would understand the bees' wings,
the bees' words blurring as they sip the dew;
and the blackbird in your throat would sing
with a voice like blackbird honey,
make morning flute-long melodious
when the distant swans and noises
of the marsh crake
break the world awake.

> Red Dragon Lady
> Green Dragon Lady

Rise up to the sky!
From the corner of my eye
I see you and smile:
Mistress, ours is the oldest master of all.

Michael Venditozzi

I LIKE IT HERE

Waiting for a break in the rain to change a tire.
Knees soaked on the gravel, putting muscle-weight
into the iron. Groan of the lug nuts, tightening.
Listening to wind roaring over the bare treetops.
Noticing the sharp red of high bush cranberries.
Watching rain spatter from eaves onto plastic leaf-bags —
maybe turning to sleet. Looking at scuffed brown shoes.

Thomas R. Smith

GOLDEN LADS

All day boys explode into the river
from a high ledge of rock. Water fields them
again and again, wraps and gilds them

in the cold shock of iron-brown petals.
It starts with a dare, a toe at the edge,
body feinting ('Go on, JUMP!'), the pool's dark

throat down there between ghostly continents
of limestone. Surely there's nothing like
that first time, throwing it away to be

reborn in a flamboyance of water.
Some run like crazy in mid-air, playing
to the gallery, most tuck their knees up,

boy-bombs, packets of pale limbs foiled in light
and a fabulous chaos of bubbles.
At night I dream of harvesting apples

and how we used to fold each unmarked fruit
in newspaper, so that murders and wars,
disasters, test scores and those blurry shots

of victims or heroes all came to this
usefulness, keeping the flesh sweet and firm.
Already the madcap boys and these heat-

struck harvest days in the Lune's rocky gorge
float off into legend, intact sweetness
wrapped in the river's quick forgetfulness.

Linda Saunders

THE MATINEE KINGS

'We are the *AY* bee *CEE-ee* MI-nors...' we sing,
sit down, lean forward in our seats and wait.
A little queue has formed at the steps leading up
to the stage. The manager stands, tuxedoed, bald,
neck reaching from his collar like the boom
of a crane. 'Harrumph.' He taps the microphone.
'All right, you three, come up. It's all your birthdays,
is it? You are?' 'Michael. And I'm TEN.' We cheer.
'And you, son?' One by one they all address
the held-out microphone as though they're drinking
from a silver cup, then he turns and bellows:
'Right, come on' — arms up conducting, sleeves
to the elbows — '*Haaappy Birthdayyyy* to you, *Haaappy...*'
'Who are we?' 'ABC Minors.' 'Who are we?'
'ABC...' 'Enjoy the show.' He strides
to the wings and waves, his spotlit shadow rippling
down the curtain as it lifts. The tunnel round
the 'Warner Brothers' logo looms and gapes
then 'Loony Tunes': Bugs Bunny bites a carrot
and we bang the arms of our chairs. *King
of The Rocket Men* begins, part nine — a flashback
chops through scenes, a shiny grown-up blonde
is carried off from bullets by a man
in dark grey overalls with rockets sparkling
from his back. She wriggles and screams. We fidget
through the kissing, then when fighting starts again
we hammer heels against our seats — warriors massing
for a battle, drumming spears against their shields.

David Penn

MY FATHER'S BOOTS

They were black, leather-soled and nail-cleated;
well-made and plain 1950s boots.
Aged twelve, ascending Lingmell in the boots
he'd had for his own school trip to the Lakes,
I was proud of their Edmund Hillary look
and stiff metal clatter. But, descending
among the wet tufts of peat-moor, a heel
fell off in the grass. My boots! — The old soles
were unlayering, like the paper tubes
of lollipops. He would have loved me to
become a priest, make the steps he'd been stopped
from taking. I knew. I wore his boots.
But the years had eaten them from inside.
I wore plastic trainers. I feel like I tried.

Thomas Jones (Dhivan)

QUEEN OF HEAVEN

Gran used to sit beneath the almost-full-sized
Pietà, the lifelike pastel-painted dead Jesus
stretched across aghast Mary's blue-robed lap.
She held up one of his limp hands gently.
Above my Gran's blue rinse his bleeding side-wound gaped.
She used to light a candle beneath them after mass,
while my brother and I, clutching big silver coins
walked in front of the pew where the Barrons sat
to the shrine to God's mother in its own small room.
Oak panelling lined it. She stood on a table,
black-robed with gold edging, an orb in one hand.
The other moved palm-out towards us. What

did I know about Mary? She was in heaven.
She had God's ear. We dropped our coins
in the black metal box and took our candles,
little-finger-thick and lilac-white. Lit, they squeezed
into four-petal iron flowers set in a sloped grid.
The light shone off the wax-heaped drip tray
and was soaked up by the black robes and the oak.
We knelt at each side. Dad stood behind us, waiting.
Around my head were rows of men's medals from both Wars.
A ship's barometer. A walking stick. Actually
I don't remember anything about the statue at all;
only the brown-lit aura of that place
and Auntie Nonie's warbling voice during mass
singing *Ave Maria* with such eager love.

Thomas Jones (Dhivan)

GOING HOME

Again you tell it:
how at five, you were not allowed
to go to the flashy brick school
on the summit of Butcher Brow,
because the rain
made the domed cobbles lethal.

Instead, you trailed
to the squat Catholic shed
on Chorley Road, and at home-time
endured the slagging of the yobs
skiving from the state school
out of reach in its sly wilderness;

and how in July
you couldn't afford the seaside
and made do with a tent
of borrowed curtain fretted with mildew
thrown over a pole on the shy margin
of the allotments;

Something in you called
for recompense. Across sixty years
you kept faith. Now, in a new estate
on the rim of a dour village
whose shortweight soil sinks
half a foot before meeting the snubs

of flint, clinker and slate;
wind-wracked and ringed with beech,
avenues of hard-nosed businessmen
and a swart, penny-pinching
butcher from Rochdale —
you stand each morning among

heights of willow herb,
damp parapets of blackberry,
harebell, and scarred valerian —
hearing hillwater seep
like a quiet scalpel through mud,
and sea birds skittering,

your shy green eyes alert
for the fitful sun glint
in fragments of glass
(pocketed years ago
on a Coronation outing to Hull)
now fallen among

cracked Jubilee plates
and a clogged watering can,

patient as the broken trove
in the clint — Alpine Violet,
Cornelian, Corallite, and sly
cloudy Obsidian.

Stephen Parr (Ananda)

ANOTHER HAPPY GRAVITY

I didn't grow up, I fell up
Onto unfolding carpets of sunshine.

Gravity can always be different,
The ground can change.

Newton on a cloud,
Receiving elevated apples;

Leaves raining backwards
Into an earth-sucking sky;

And us, listening down to the birds
Burrowing happily under the rocks.

Padmakara (Roger Bygott)

MIDGIE MATRIX

r= raindrops
m=midgie
a=air

rararammmmmmm
rmmmmraraaaaam
rammmmmmrarmr
rararmmmrramaar

(This poem may be read diagonally, horizontally, vertically or hysterically).

Sheena Blackhall

STILL

Two dragonflies thumb the air
like flickerbooks. All morning

I listen to their transparent oracle.
They hover and swoop, make

their own circles over the water,
ripples in dense air. Then

they find each other, collide
and dive, dancing and beautiful.

They look as if they should be singing.
They are air and time and this love

that seems to keep happening. *Still*.
Am I watching them or are they

watching me? What time would it be
if we were dragonflies,

just one summer to tinge
with our quick bronze wings?

Linda France

DAYFLY

Three hundred-millionths of a second.
If that's how long one particle lasts
think how endless one day is.
You think a day's too short?
Greedy thing.

Ko Un
translated by Brother Anthony of Taizé and Young-Moo Kim.

THE MIRACLE

Remember that fantastic spider's web?
Fantastic less as feature than as feat
of structural engineering that had stretched
the top thread, measuring some ten metres,
from one tip of our neighbour's pampas grass
to a branch halfway up our almond tree.
An invisible drawbridge spanned the twin front paths.
Its height gave clearance; we passed underneath
a miracle, just going in and out of doors.
The web hung where steps started and paths stopped.
Lack of disturbance meant it had the chance
to grow huge and round, like a firework, or
a station clock, and grant us love's whole sequence:
discovery, unforeseen endurance, shock.

Julia Lewis

THE SCENT OF DECAYED APPLES
in the desk drawer
is a wall of stars
and shining shimmering dust.
MOTTLED SOUNDS
M

U

S

T

SPEAK
to the bare mildewed feet
of Kannon's ineffable hearing.
The pink plum blossoms decorating
each perfect realm
drip big rain drops
to
the
concrete sidewalk.
Shoe soles and earthworms
move through the puddles
and mud.
It is all
QUICK
while the bell rings
through the incense.

Michael McClure

INTO THE SILENCE

IS THERE SOME KIND OF BIRDSONG

Is there some kind of birdsong
inside your breast?
My ear approaches your breast.

Ko Un
translated by Brother Anthony of Taizé and Young-Moo Kim.

INTO THE SILENCE

If ever I don't reply
it is the stillness that has taken me
from you. It kisses me when I'm tired,
when there are no more questions to be asked.

If ever I don't reply
it is because the only answer left is silence.

If ever I don't reply
it is the stillness kissing my tired eyes,
taking me away from you
into the silence.

If ever my tired eyes kiss your questions
with silence, please don't reply.

Rachael Boast

LISTENING OUTSIDE

At night our listening outside, our straining to see
in the monochrome dark, changes us, like ink
spreading through a glass of water, so we become

something of the night, our senses heightened,
and wary of the sounds of other creatures padding
under the hedge or clacking through the trees.

And when we come into the house, we notice
the difference, readjust to the light, and the familiar
rows of herbs and spices, shelves and chairs,

have themselves become strange. Here, there's no need
for keen senses, we let them go. In ten minutes
we've almost forgotten the difference,

and if we do remember, it's a memory whose content
we can't re-enter. A thick coat dulls our touch, our hearing,
our sight — protects yet distances us from the world.

Like returning to our parents' house after a summer holiday
or after years as an adult, the walls and furnishings
reassuringly familiar but strange. We sink into our old bed,

and have feelings as familiar as words on the tip
of our tongue. 'Now why is this so familiar', we ask,
'so comforting and after a time, so contracting?'

Tony McKeown

HABIT

The shoes put on each time
left first, then right.

The morning potion's teaspoon
of sweetness stirred always
for seven circlings — no fewer, no more —
into the cracked blue cup.

Touching the pocket for wallet,
for keys,
before closing the door.

How did we come
to believe these small rituals' promise,
that we are today the selves we yesterday knew,
tomorrow will be?

How intimate and unthinking,
the way the toothbrush is shaken dry after use,
the part we wash first in the bath.

Which habits we learned from others
and which are ours alone we may never know.
Unbearable to acknowledge
how much they are themselves our fated life.

Open the travelling suitcase —

There the beloved red sweater,
bright tangle of necklace, earrings of amber.
Each confirming: I chose these, I.

But habit is different: it chooses.
And we, its good horse,
opening our mouths at even the sight of the bit.

Jane Hirshfield

SHOES

A girl in a loose pink jumper is stroking a man's hands lovingly.
The man, leaning forward, has his eyes closed, as though stunned.
It is dusk.

The mud paths of the afternoon have wandered into vagueness.
The blind earth
plunges into unknown space, held by nothing.

I have finished my self-appointed tasks:
buying fruit-juice, having a haircut,
looking at shoes.

On the wall a man's pink hands are frozen
forever above a keyboard.
Overnight the patterned season has been obliterated.

In dim light
I tread the stairs hesitantly, hearing the caged beat
of my shoes on wood.

Stephen Parr (Ananda)

THAT SUMMER

The room filled with pale blue light:
the same sash window that sliced my thumb
wide open onto the silent street.

After hours of not sleeping, I came to you,
rocked you awake, said 'I want you
to come to my bed.'

I was surprised the glass did not shatter:
it fell so quickly it took a minute
for me to notice. I stood

looking out at a whitewashed wall, a boundary
of wagon-wheels on the far roadside —
buried to their axles, their shadows turning

slowly across the wall. Blood ran
to my fingertips, dripped
onto the frame: too sudden for pain.

We travelled far that night, beyond
our bodies' dumb pronouncements, stimulus
and response.

It had already happened. I could do nothing
but free myself, and wonder
how suddenly the summer had ended,

how wide the roads were in that small town.

Ian Tromp (Manjusura)

THE HOUSE ON FREMONT STREET

In July heat, the full moon edges in and out
of clouds. Breezes softly riffle the pages
of oak leaves. Frog voices thrum on the river.

What was once our path along the shore is now
a paved walk. New streetlamps blur the humid air.
And here's our old house in its yard of lilacs

and moonbeams, where twenty years ago tonight
you invited me to your bed, the rain
that had driven us indoors spangling the dark. . .

I've carried that first night so long in memory,
converted it grain by grain as an earth-
worm converts earth, it's becoming spirit.

I look at your face that shone then for me
in the drenched starlight. We were buds packed
with the selves we'd unfold to each other.

Blessings on the lovers! Inside someone's still up,
window lit, floating. It's someone else's house now
to pretend it's solid and not a dream at all!

Thomas R. Smith

A QUESTION OF LOVE

I listened to you making supper in the kitchen, the sound of the cooker
competes with the football on the radio, and loses. Your world seems so
complete behind that door or maybe just completely yours. For a while I
resist the temptation to disturb you, but the desire is strong and when I
finally step in it surprises us both — no reason, just to see you so at
home in your life.

After supper I wash the dishes, an action you always delight in. I
study a saucepan, still full of food, and I follow my normal course of
action, yet I know a hidden message will expose me. I decant the food
and wash the pan, it's a sensible choice as the pan will only burn if re-
heated again. Oh, but the sweetness of that action won't lie down, like a
thread it hangs loose, I can't tie it away.

Later on, I hear you in the kitchen, reassembling your life, the
thread catches you and ties itself neatly around you. You recognise

yourself in my action and wonder how you found me. So many actions sent out in the world that you never thought to get a reply. You recognise the message, but I am nonchalant in the face of discovery — it was just sensible, reasonable and ordinary — but you maintain it as an act of love.

Afterwards I wonder about that love. Where is it to be found if not in acts of kindness where you step slightly beyond necessity and give a bit more. Where is it to be found if not in that which is sensible, reasonable and ordinary.

Saddhanandi

HORSES AT CHRISTMAS

In our little house Creedence were singing
about the old cotton fields, the baby
was flat on his back in front of the fire,
eyes swimming with flame.
Christmas morning, and you were at church.
I thought of going to join you late,
but instead took the baby up to the horses.
Out in the field he started crying.
Maybe I should have taken him to the bath
of stone, the discipline of a saviour, the sanctuary
of hymns —
                    But the horses saved us.
To be close to them, so tough and nothing
to do with us, and their breathing all over him,
and the flaking mud on their necks
where they had rolled, and the sucking of hooves
as they walked the sodden field.
The horses with their long heads
watched us watch them.
Then they turned, drumming the field,

leaving us alone — the damp morning
all about, the soaked grass under foot,
the baby's diaphanous ears going pink in the cold
as silence bowed back to earth.

Henry Shukman

SIX SUBSTITUTES FOR LOVE

the white suede inside a peanutshell

the deep V of a gingko leaf

the indigo pollen of a blue anemone

the bitter juice in a bowl of black olives

the lips of a trumpet player

city lights on the horizon

Linda France

THE BELL

It is worth listening
to the sound of a bell,
the resonance rolling through space
as if on a carpet of steel
extending from the invisible,
shocking with the sound of the real
like an angel's immensity intruding upon us;

the first and last of languages
hammered into air,
a shrill awakening of the wordless
unforgiving alphabet of nails,
turning the sky into bronze,
turning the air into gardens of alarms,
cutting the clouds with its declaration
of the bitter knowledge of the iron fruit.
A knell for the not quite living, perhaps,
for those whose mouths are as cold as a bell.
The sound of that which is definite,
defying the reason of doubt,
ringing all too loud, perhaps,
with the kind of acute simplicity
we hope will one day save us.

It is worth looking closely at the shape of a bell,
like the armour of unknown space,
a perverse cup for the sun, perhaps,
keeping it cold,
a womb in the mother of metal
offering nothing desire can hold
like a dome in the midst of air,
a temple or a tomb for the most austere
unreturning heart.

But I fear being constrained by its promises.
I fear being captive beneath the weight
of a chilling perfection.
I hold the bell still in my hand
and feel the power of a cold restraint
stirring within.
Then I see the tongue hanging
in the golden mouth,
corpse like, chained, unsettled,
tied to the womb that prolongs its birth

in a frozen sensuous devotion.
And I see the vanity of all expression!
I hear the anger of the injured word!
How every gesture once performed
compels itself to endless repetition,
with every breath of our yearning
clamouring against the fathomless,
labouring on and on towards eternal fixation,
a relentless rhythm of reluctant steel,
an inconclusive invention!
How I both love and fear
that which is distinct!

But how that noise torments me!
Like blows on the anvil
I no longer control!
Longing for a sound to destroy all others!
For one sensation to cast its shadow
over the world!
Longing for that which cannot calm
the howling,
unable to speak
in any other language than its own!
To cry in cold syllables
like someone stuck
on the slopes of his own
sheer sonority!

What words could ever match
the sound of a bell?
I can think of just a few:
'longing', 'desire', 'obsession';
a few words whose tone torments us,
whose incessant clatter compels us on!
Penetrating the rest of our speech,
tearing apart our ideas,
drowning out whatever else

we might have wanted to say!
A few words which resonate
for long, long hours,
fading only in their own time,
if ever;
a few words which have had to hover
above the rest of language,
as if trying to imitate an ultimate voice,
a constant music constantly heard,
but one which is not yet finished,
one which is not yet really understood.

Sasanaratna

WITHOUT SKYLARKS

Then I noticed silence,
    risen above the skyline
        like an invisible forest
which surrounded me
    now with its motionless
        unseen leaves.

I'd climbed out of all sound:
    barkings and bleatings of the valley,
        whine of a chainsaw,
business of crows
    (& news 'as it happens',
        the static of war).

Even the fleeting twitter
    of a pippit seemed forbidden
        this high theatre
of silence founded

in the deep granaries
    of the fells.

It slowed me, stopped
    the thud of my blood, stilled
        my breath, as I sank
into it,
    stretched out
        on the grassy shoulder of Green Bell.

And I heard how silence can toll
    as the hills all around
        take up the tone,
which issues from their old long throats:
    such patience
        in earth and stone.

Linda Saunders

SAME CHAIR SAME WINDOW

I

Copper beech arrested 'en volant', form moving out and away
    from the vertical. Tilt of the branches down towards
    down until, ground
    comme petticoat flounces
    hides as most private of places
    the birthpoint — emergence from root as trunk.

Aubergine-black and shiny foliage — slender uppers more sparing.
    The middle-mass, where it reflects the sky,
    each leaf glazed white with opacity
    like a thickening eye.
    Daubed maroon darkness.
    Darkness marooned on a three-tier band of colour —

Bright green, smoke blue, dense white. That is: light-giving lawn,
    far hills and sky. At its foot
    a miniature wilderness: feathery grasses,
    long-stemmed polkadot buttercups
    left by the mower as more properly owed
    to the tree's benedicite, its above-ground circumference.

A largesse of silence fills the perceptual space. No callers
    except for one or two martins late to bed
    (it is late but light; far north, and midsummer).
    There must be breeze or the tree's outreaches
    would not breathe as they do — slight shift,
    slight lift and fall, most obvious high against white.

And then nothing. Still as a painting. A pale moth jitters into purple.
    The tree's whole form remains as if splattered
    from one spun axis; single branches
    hold a delicate balance, mimicking
    the far hills' curves but more arched, like royal hands
    knuckled and raised for lips to bend to.

II

The birds — they can't be still at their dawn salutation, can they?
Yet I think they are, for the background's a serried gauze
hemmed in by the opposite mountain. Far-reaching chirrup
indistinguishable from, underneath it, the rush of a burn.
Let my ears rest on this (their full weight) with fearlessness.
Buttercups still asleep.

Now, as my ears explore this vent through the sounding world,
trying to write silently so as not to break the ear's venture,
I gather surprise at how distinct the words are, motoring
through my head, usually unnoticed. Who would have
thought it? But if I'm listening to words like 'curtain' can I really
be hearing *birds*?

Such pleasure in edgework hearkening. Echo and resonance.
Shapes of space made known through the auditory halo
of birds' cadenzas, with approximate mass of foliage
and today's air's water-content. I don't mean anything
whimsical. The human ear's a batlike, radar organ; we don't
give it credit.

As the birds one by one desist, raindrops are hundred by hundred
audible. Colourless items — visible as down-moving strands
against darker backgrounds by virtue of mini reflections.
Against the pale shin of the larch they're not visible at all. Their sound
is a crackling, like fire. On copper-beech leaves however, the rain
most definitely slaps.

Now birds are quiet I can believe the old legend that rain
makes a rattle of grass. I keep wanting to repeat the word for the thing
like a mind-fingered bead — *rain*, *lawn*, — flying like birds from piazza to
     niches
to take up old places in songs of belonging.
I write *It is raining here — the softest of drums on the lawn —*
Edward Thomas'

still-falling next-morning rain on Auden's long-vacated lawn.
Is it wrong to leave this window (which doesn't belong to me)
open? Probably. View, my view. Not mine though. Now
you are quietening through ninety degrees. Now you are wholly
glass-intervened. I am leaving today, with my blue and red rucksack.

Julia Lewis

DISTANT LIGHT

[UNTITLED]

It's cold.
It's the mind.

Ko Un translated by Brother Anthony of Taizé and Young-Moo Kim.

DISTANT LIGHT

Me and Cynthia — that's my mom — we're sitting on the couch drinking tea. We're drinking tea because she doesn't have any money to buy beer these days, and neither do I, even though I think we'd both really like a beer right now.

I've been telling her about this crazy physics stuff they're coming out with, about how they've figured out that light takes the form of either a particle or a wave depending on whether or not it's being watched. Yeah. And that affects the path it travels because then it either bounces off objects or bends around them. Well, actually, that's old news now, but the crazy thing is, they've also figured out: that this means when you look at star, you affect the way that star's light travels, but that light has been traveling for billions of years. The star you're looking at may not even exist anymore. So, you're actually effecting the way that light traveled in the past. Yeah.

Which pretty much fucks up the whole way we've been thinking about time and space and consciousness. And everything.

So my mother listens to all of this and thinks it's pretty amazing and all, and then — she's just quiet for awhile and doesn't even drink her tea, and then she's like, 'You know, I was just thinking. If that's all true, then it's also like, if you look at events in the past and think about them from where you are, you kind of change them. So I can look back at leaving you and your sister when you were kids, and even though it's so long ago it's not as far back as that starlight, so maybe we can kind of go back and change it just by looking at it. Wouldn't that be nice, Jer, if we could go back and change that now, just by you and me sitting here talking about it and being together and wanting it to be different? Maybe it doesn't have to be so tough.'

And she looked at me and I swear, her face was, like, twenty five years old just then, the way I remember her when we lived in the little brown house on Maple when I was six and my sister was seven and Mom used to read *Little House on the Prairie* to us and if we went to bed on time she'd stay up and make us little rag dolls or something and we'd wake up and they'd be on the pillow next to us, just a little rag doll sewn out of an old t-shirt or something, but we though it was so cool and we never realized how late she must have stayed up to make them even though she had to work all day the next day washing dishes at the bakery and she must have been tired but I never saw her tired and there was just the one time when she sat in the bathtub and cried and wouldn't stop and my sister and I got scared and got the neighbor woman who sat on the edge of the tub and talked really quiet to my mother and said stuff like 'red light, green light' that didn't make any sense, and we watched from the doorway and were scared and I knew that it was because we wouldn't behave but I didn't know how to be better and pretty soon my sister and I drove out to the country with our aunt and stayed for a few weeks and then she sat us down one morning and told us that we wouldn't be going back to live with our mother, and I lay on my bed afterward and cried for the whole afternoon and nobody could do anything to make me stop.

And we saw her on weekends sometimes after, and she'd take us to go see a movie downtown — not some stupid kid's movie, but a real adult movie, like *Gallipoli* or *Pennies from Heaven* or *Ragtime*, and after we'd go to her apartment by the library and listen to Joni Mitchell records and we'd talk and it was nice, but then we'd go back home to the farm and my chest would be all hollow and scooped out and I wouldn't know why because I was just a fucking kid, man, and you don't know why or what to do about it.

And it was only years later that I found out that she wanted us back, but she was too scared to ask her sister to give us back, so she didn't. She just thought about us all the time, and cried in her bed, too, and eventually she met another guy and had more kids with him, but she didn't forget about us and even though she loved her other kids, they didn't take our place. Our place was still there somewhere inside of her.

137

So here we are, twenty years later, me and my Mom, who I call Cynthia now, sitting on her old brown couch holding Salvation Army cups full of chamomile tea and talking, and she looks twenty five again and I realize something. So I say 'Cynthia?' and she says, 'Hmmm?' and I say, 'What you said just now about being able to go back and change things by looking at them?' and she says, 'Yeah?' and I say, 'Maybe it's not such a crazy idea.' And she looks at me with her young face and she has a puzzled little smile and she says, 'What do you mean?' and I don't know how to tell her what I see, so I just say, 'Nothing, Mom. I love you.' And we finish drinking our tea.

Jeremy Glenn

THE ORCHID FLOWER

Just as I wonder
whether it's going to die,
the orchid blossoms

and I can't explain why it
moves my heart, why such pleasure

comes from one small bud
on a long spindly stem, one
blood red gold flower

opening at mid-summer,
tiny, perfect in its hour.

Even to a white-
haired craggy poet, it's
purely erotic,

pistil and stamen, pollen,
dew of the world, a spoonful
of earth, and water.

Erotic because there's death
at the heart of birth,

drama in those old sunrise
prisms in wet cedar boughs,

deepest mystery
in washing evening dishes
or teasing my wife,

who grows, yes, more beautiful
because one of us will die.

Sam Hamill

NASTURTIUM LEAVES

The long stalks tender and submissive; the leaf-platters
    proffered, singular,
handed-up not heart-shaped but partaking of heart-shapédness.

Cool greens, white-veined, surround the hot flash-flares of the flower
    and
nodding and trembling, protect her reputation.

The position of stalk to leaf is as pole to parasol though not
    so central
or like a waiter's dish held high through a crowded café

and on the leaf-side
    (seen side)
dots mark the meeting-place of stalk and leaf

like towns on an island map, a single eye
    white-blind; blind-white
with radial veins to the edges. Though it trembles

the leaf is secure, held by a secret stay,
      an esteem,
pinch-fastened at a back-point of balance.

Held-forth faces tipped like children's: you can see young
      girls, carrying
their seen breasts like this, all summer, with their unseen thoughts.

Julia Lewis

IT WAS A FROST–STRUCK CHRYSANTHEMUM

It was a frost-struck chrysanthemum. Such was her beginning.
It was a dew-soaked peony. Such was her end.

Today too she was a flower's beginning and its end.

Ko Un translated by Brother Anthony of Taizé and Young-Moo Kim.

QUIDDITY

If I could redesign desire,
that magnetic stare
would lose its potency

And small things
which can't be owned
would unlock me,

Like last night's rain
poised in a leaf hand;
a pure sphere of light and water.

Varasahaya

MYSTERIOSO E I G H T

BLACK ARISEN TO BLACK ROSES IS VOICES
BETWEEN PETALS.
The yellow centers with anthers
B
E
G
I
N

WITH BLACK.
Lonely. Sweet as honey.
Overpopulated by blossoms and petals.
Consciousness narrowly streams
like a nematode, muscularly,
between plastics and hunks
OF MANUFACTURED THOUGHT.
Through births of new hatreds
– poisonous as ever.
Greedy for ignorance
as a sitcom.

And we stretch
in this bed
touching shoulders
just as whales and mice
do.

Michael McClure

PETALS

Petals
Of the lilac, petals
From mauve and white plumes from
Orchard appleblossom foamy behind
Brick walls from
Gnarled grey branches green lofty
Crowns from
Manycandled chestnut, petals
Of hawthorn plum pear cherry rambling
Rose bushrose bougainvillea elder lime rowan, petals
Dropping on running water, on sunlit silent
Green scum, pink and white
Confetti on gleaming black car-roofs, petals
Borne over ancient chimneys, swept
Down dim avenues, falling
Like rain like seed like swansdown flying
Like spindrift against blue sky like whiteflock
Dawnbirds, petals
Tossed scattered whirling spiralling, littered
Down loamy furrows, sticking
To mudcaked boots, petals
Blowing into eyes hair hands, drifting
Over naked bodies of lovers, collecting
In crimson pools, in purple heaps, pink
Streams along country roads, rivers
Of petals to the horizon, rising
Tide of petals throughout the world flooding
Earth surging into the sky cloudburst
Apocalypse of petals Spring's
Manifesto of petals poet's
Signature of petals red
Petals.

Sangharakshita

CLEMATIS

It goes out of her head the moment
she thinks of it;
she wanders from room to room trying

to work out what to cook for tea;
she loses her red box
of thread and darning needles.

She remembers the shine
on the crushed velvet
she embroidered for her first dance

but what the man said yesterday
about the fused washing machine
is beyond her.

She watches the blackbirds feed:
her horizon is the two-foot lattice fence
laced with birch light.

She rests; the lifelong snubs
of words like *taxi, cocktail, theatre,
garage,* are fading out; she's rising

above them, a dark-haired figure
slipping nightly through the grass
to her woody shrine:

a trickle of spring
water, leaf-mould, clematis —
a few veined stars quivering

Stephen Parr (Ananda)

EGG-TIMERS

Already there's the odd day when
friends become blanks: names frozen solid,
their voices sadly accusing beyond bends

in the morning. Is this how *insane*
begins, that final mangled blackness with no end?
No, this is only *age*, small things letting go

that distort the tuning of this miraculous engine,
a vagueness merely. But then
there are the words and places I've known since childhood,

like *marmalade* and *Liverpool* that inexplicably
aren't there. And the name of a friend's cat
utterly unreachable. What helps is finding a mnemonic:

rave for David, *plane* for Jet.
Yet I can't escape the fact that something's escaping
from the zoo my mind is slowly turning into.

And lurking in the corner's what some buff said on the radio
(was it years or days ago?) that really kick-starts the panic:
something foreign that sounds like egg timers.

Stephen Parr (Ananda)

OLD GENT

How you get to be an old gent
is not by choice, not, that is,
by deliberation or design.
One year a stick to steady the walking

144

then a cap to protect the bald head
A jacket is required for pockets
to put things in, keys, purse,
spectacle case, wallet.
Before you know it
you are a rare sight
in your street, a foreign object
to the children on their way
to school.

Terry Diffey

THE OLD LADY

In 1985, my mate at University had lank yellow hair and wore a studded
jacket. He walked hunched in off-white trainers, and liked to be called
Sid. He called me *Man*, which I relished.

Passing through London, we had arranged to meet a recent
acquaintance of mine. Jeremy kept his hair in a backswept mop, like
Jeremy Irons. He wore brogues and lived in a comfortable Brixton
garret. We were joined by Daniel, elegant and half-black. They were
students at Goldsmith's College of Art. They twinkled and informed us
that they had prepared an outing for our benefit.

Within the hour we had arrived at the back door of an antiquated
medical college, where simple art materials were thrust upon us. The
technician at the Mortuary was a big man with cropped hair. He was
friendly with Jeremy and Daniel, but cast a suspicious glance at Sid and
Me.

So. Are you from Goldsmith's too?

We mumbled our yesses, and flapped our newly-acquired sketch-
books. The man looked troubled for a second, then seemed to shrug
internally. What did it matter if we were not art students? He could
handle any misconduct arising.

He showed us into the wide, dim room. There was more than one body in there, but only one was uncovered, at the head. The Old Lady.

Scott looked even paler. Jeremy and Daniel were feigning normality. We pulled stacking chairs into a semi-circle around the corpse. My first corpse.

We acted as if we meant business. A rectangular incision had been applied to her face and neck. The skin had been peeled down to the table. Inside were tendons, muscles, veins: pale and bloodless: This was just a dead body. I found this aperture less disturbing than the oddness of her hair, which had been shaved down to a white stubble on that side of the head, the rest remaining curly in the standard Old-Lady style. Thoughts of permission came to me. Who had permitted this?

Jeremy had begun work with a set of ovoids, assigning a system of latitudes and longitudes to the space occupied by her head. Using a sky-blue pencil, Daniel was looping his paper, non-stop, iterating towards the best lines. Upon these he pressed harder, and her likeness began to swell from his page. I was impressed — they could really sketch. Scott was making a peaky effort, like one of the 'before' pictures from *Drawing on the Right Side of the Brain*. Very Left-Sided. Very Heriott-Watt Computer Science Department. Very small-town Scotland. Very *what the* fuck *am I doin' here?*

I imagined her adult children: a sober businessman and a sensible, sensitive woman with teenagers of her own. I imagined that they could see me and understand the foolishness that had led me into this intimacy with their Mother's body. I tried to do her justice, both with my rendering and my attitude. I let the pencil guide my hand, and she drifted into focus for me too. I began to enjoy a vigil with respect to the Old Lady. By degrees, and softly like the sounds of slithering graphite, I was beyond resenting Jeremy's prank or fearing the technician working in the adjoining rooms.

Our man was cheerier as we left: either his mood had brightened, or my paranoia had eased.

We've got one of the PG Chimps in here. From the PG Tips adverts.

He did not offer a viewing of this rare subject; just a fact from another day on the job. And we were out: on the street, under the sky, free and alive.

Bruce Peterkin

BIRDS

My grandmother carried her burden
for thirty years, then one afternoon
as she carried her shopping home
it lifted off her *like a bird – just like that,*
she said the one time she mentioned it.
The last time we met she wasn't ackled
right all afternoon. She pointed
to some rooks above the telly that I had
to say weren't there; her mind dispersing,
lifting away from her. When the vicar said
Ashes, I cried into my palms, very quietly.

Subhadassi

VIVA LA VIDA

Every day she glances at the mysterious flowers in a neighbour's
backyard. She is new to the area and the hidden, waist-high flowers
fascinate her. They are bagged like woolen clothes to protect them from
moths.

For months she's wondered what plant the owner is shielding under
upended garbage bags loosely looped with string. Then one morning
the plastic is gone. Finally released are arum lilies growing out of the
damp, wet earth. Lilies beloved of graveyards and bogs and murals
painted by Diego Rivera. Funeral lilies she loathes and fears.

Her ill father swims in front of her, holding an armful of pitcher-
shaped flowers. The white shroud of the blossoms is the Hindu colour
not of purity, but of sorrow and the spiked stamens are the mourning
yellow of the ancient Egyptians. The huge bouquet of arum lilies emerge
from the ground like a delivery of flowers for the forward dead.

A believer in solar winds, long-tailed comets and omens, she knows these lilies are harbingers of disaster. She knows this with the certainty of a clairvoyant seeing letters and numbers soon to be carved on her dying father's headstone.

Frida Kahlo's last defiant painting was executed eight days before her death. Bedridden and in great pain, she chose as her subject the most beloved Mexican fruit: watermelons. Whole, halved, serrated, sliced, in blood-red oils she lovingly depicted the lusciousness of their dying flesh. Should anyone miss her meaning, she painted in capital letters on the glistening pulp of the wedge nearest the viewer, *VIVA LA VIDA*.

Her father eating watermelon in the garden, newspapers spread over the table. The rind of his watermelon discoloured with disease, but the heart inside is red and sweet. He scrapes out the shiny, black seeds with a fork. If a stray finds it way into his mouth, he spits it into the dirt for the birds.

As juice runs from his mouth, he admires the beauty of the morning lilies planted under the pecan tree. Though this will be his last summer, his voice is like a boy's: full of awe and wonder at the new flowers on their slender stalks. He points out how they all lean out from beneath their leaf canopy, eager to catch the afternoon sun.

Her love for him, the hugeness of it, fills her eyes. He is the tent pole that holds up the sky. Like Frida, courageous in the face of death, even as these terrifying blossoms trumpet his extinction.

Anne Aylor

'IN THE WOODS ARE MANY MORE'

Selling wild orchids at my door one day
A man said, 'In the woods are many more...
Deep in the gloom, high on the thickset trees,
Wild orchids hang like clouds of butterflies,
Golden and white, spotted with red and black,
As huge as birds, or tiny as a bee,
Wild orchids which no eye has ever seen

148

Save ours, who wander in these rich green glooms
All day throughout the year.' I bought his sprays,
Paid him, and bore them in; and as I went
My eyes by chance fell on a shelf of books, —
The Buddha's Teachings, — and thereafter glanced
Up to the Buddha's image as He smiled
Above them from the alcove. Strange it was
That, as my eyes from book to image passed,
Dwelling an instant on that calm, pure Face,
There, with the frail cold blossoms in my hands,
The words that man spoke at my door should ring
Through my stilled heart again and yet again
Like music — 'In the woods are many more...'

Sangharakshita

HOW ARE WE TO SAY GOODBYE?

SNOWY MORNING

When we were nine or ten and used to play
at dying — hands clasped to the chest,
Goodbye, beautiful world, I love you! —
we didn't believe it could ever really be done.

Say goodbye to *everything*? A gunshot wound
in 'Alias Smith and Jones' could set us thinking —
please *please* don't die — or a feathered mess
that had been a pigeon squashed on the road.

Even Divinity class, that final sponge of vinegar
on a speartip. Goodbye, beautiful vinegar.
Now, under the shag of decades, after so much
contact with things, it takes a morning like this.

Snow has fallen, a light crust. On the white field
green trails zigzag where the horses wandered,
a crazy scribble shows where they fed.
There they are now, two statues stooping.

All the ewes are sitting, thawing their grass.
Puddles crunch like caramel. Little snowfalls
crumble down a hedge. The silver-birch
trembles in its own twigs' shadows.

And under the rusty chestnut I walk
through a rain of crystals. There isn't much to say.
This is a day that decides by itself to be beautiful.
This field is a bride. How are we to say goodbye?

Henry Shukman

WORDS FOR JACOB

That fox I glimpsed in New Hampshire
runs across your page — a diary entry
from the untamed world.

Down on the shore we gather treasure:
only white things, you say, and blue sea-
glass, and this one tiny shell shaped like a hand.

Walking back home in the eye of cold
you describe your favourite poem: a boy
like you finds a beautiful rose that never dies.

Overnight the snow has cracked open
the neighbourhood. The cars prowl past,
suspicious. Why should I walk so joyously
  to the clouded train?

David Keefe (Manjusvara)

THE HEART AS ORIGAMI

Each one has its shape.
For love, two sleeping ducks.
For selfless courage, the war horse.
For fear of death, the daylily's one-day flower.
More and more creased each year, worn paper thin,
and still it longs for them all.
Not one of the lives of this world the heart does not choose.

Jane Hirshfield

FIRST LIGHT

First light, touching these bricks
as if they were the skin of the world;

fingers of gold, stroking
their weathered chalk-grey forms;

so I imagine it is when grace
finally enters the mind

and plays with all those old
worn out desires

as if they were child's toys —
the building blocks of the world.

Ratnagarbha

TOWER DREAM

Last night
they swept across my sleep:

floating, falling women
like leaves drifting
across blue September sky.

Secretaries, lawyers,
businesswomen: one delicately
arranges her skirt,

another holds a closed umbrella
firmly pointing down.

Mary Clark (Amarapuspa)

WHERE I WAS WHEN IT HAPPENED
for Tim Zoom & Dayavajra

About to leave their house,
and fill the car with cheap supermarket fuel,
I was arrested by my friends' cry,
the two of them kneeling on the floor
hunched over the radio, as if trying to appease
what was already incomprehensible,
while the story continued to break live on the air.

The second attempt I drove in radio-silence.
At the supermarket there were no outward signs.
Yet everything being read in the cafe behind the immaculate glass
had in a flash been reduced to yesterday's news.
How could I tell them — those innocent figures
sitting so calm in the dust-free air — what was ghost-
written on the dying autumn sunlight?

David Keefe (Manjusvara)

LOS ANGELES AIRPORT GHAZAL

Reading Ghalib in the shadows of the neon.
Across the runway the airlines screaming their names in neon.

The arrivals and departures fill the coloured screens
with an unearthly glow, like the moon, in the shadows of the neon.

Children play, to them it is all the same. Phosphorescent
baggage tags comically teasing the shadows of the neon.

In the bookshop Rumi is shelved under 'New Age' —
a thousand years of history re-written in the shadows of the neon.

And although it isn't spoken, death is in the air,
others seeing ruin in America's shadows of the neon.

David Keefe (Manjusvara)

THE MONK STOOD BESIDE A WHEELBARROW

The monk stood beside a wheelbarrow, weeping.

God or Buddha nowhere to be seen —
these tears were fully human,
bitter, broken,
falling onto the wheelbarrow's rusty side.

They gathered at its bottom,
where the metal drank them in to make more rust.

You cannot know what you do in this life, what you have done.

The monk stood weeping.
I knew I also had a place on this hard earth.

Jane Hirshfield

THE END OF THE SENTENCE

The thing which I fear most
is the end of the sentence.
The little dot like a star reversed.
The little dot like a hole in space.
The little dot that kills.
A simple sentence such as, *I am a Jew*.

and almost a million lives are lost per letter.
The little dot which makes each judgement final.

The hard word hammered in the dreaming hand
honours the barbs of language.
The broken word which lets us fall;
honours our escape
though the cold floor of the steady world
always seems to return.

Now I know why poets like Celan
leave their sentences incomplete.
While others look to certainty
to save themselves,
I put my faith in its absence,
in the open, the ever unformed.
I desire to unstate the obvious,
to unsteady the world.

Sasanaratna

SCATTERING THE ASHES

At last the rain cleared and we found a barley-field
where the crop was knee-high, and in our town shoes
paced the lumpy furrows along the edge
until our trousers were soaked. My brother held it out,
open, and I pushed my hand in. It was like
dark corn, or oatmeal, or both, the fine dust
surprisingly heavy as it sighed through the green
blades and hit the earth. And like the sower
in that nursery picture ('To bed with the lamb,
and up with the laverock') we strode on, flinging it
broadcast, left and right, out over the field.

And there was no doubt that things were all in their places,
the tumbled clouds moving back, light in the wheel-ruts
and puddles of the lane as we walked to the car;
and yes, there were larks scribbling their songs on the sky
as the air warmed up. We noticed small steps
by a pool in the stream where a boy might have played
and people fetched water once, and wild watercress
that streamed like green hair inside the ribbed gloss of the current.
And then I was swinging the wheel as we found our way
round the lane corners in a maze of tall hedges
patched with wild roses, under steep slopes of larch
and sycamore, glimpsing the red sandstone of castles
hidden high in the woods. And the grit under our nails
was the midpoint of a spectrum that ran from the pattern in our cells
to the memories of two children, and it was all right.

Grevel Lindop

VESSEL

There was so little left of your father
on the night he died: he was reduced
to a heaving need for air.
We sat with him and talked as he breathed
and I didn't think how astonishing it was
that we could do these two things at once,
talking and breathing, at ease
in air's familiar medium,
taking it in and cutting it up for words,
while he worked so hard
just to get enough of it.
Speaking of the moment of death
Tibetans say it's like the breaking of a vase:
the air inside and the air outside
are mingled, becoming one.

The body, like the shattering sides of the vase
falls away, and there's no difference anymore
no wall to keep the world apart
nor boundary to hold him in
his confusion and pain gone in a moment
his breath dissolving into air
and his room
our bodies and breath
our low voices
and the lamplight
and our love and his
for just a few seconds
suddenly one.

Ian Tromp (Manjusura)

LEAVING PRAYER
After Faiz Ahmed Faiz

What certainty in miracles?
I have none. Yet, when the shadows
and dreams of this great world
are no longer mine,
when I no longer glimpse you
in the mask of strange cities,
I still hope to return one last time
and stand by your door,
to be certain someone is with you
sharing your torment,
your smallest pain. Only then,

Only then will I be free to depart
— never to return —
for the unknown direction.

Based on the English translation by Agha Shahid Ali of the Faiz Ahmed Faiz poem 'Desire'.
David Keefe (Manjusvara)

WRITING POETRY AT EDINBURGH AIRPORT

Li Po said, 'To read poems is to be alive twice.'
At the airport it is easier to see how everyone is equal.
There is only one human story: it ends in leaving.

David Keefe (Manjusvara)

TOWARDS A NEW RENAISSANCE

Dear friend with the crescent moon above your door,
I have heard that you are overcome by poetry,

that you are afloat somewhere inside the world's great
sorrow, with the language of love as your compass.

You have been gone a long time, a white sail
full of the clear sky, and no land in sight.

One such as you will become an ocean unto itself
because you learn and live your craft well.

Don't forget to report back to us — I have a feeling
the universal winds are sensitive to words.

Rachael Boast

DARK

Some day we will all go out
into the dark.
No, not the darkness of death
or despair that all of us fear,
the great dark, the good dark
the darkness that waits at your door
like a huge patient cat,
purring, wanting to be let in,
wanting you to touch its belly
that is everywhere
outside your door
tonight and every night.

Ratnagarbha

TEA HOUSE

I've lost track of the hours that have
passed since I first saw you in here,
your face bowed to pen and page.

This place always writes your name
at the bottom of my cup. What can I say?
Not that I miss you, for presence and absence

have become the same thing. Perhaps just this —
that even though you're somewhere on the other
side of the globe, we're travelling together.

I just wanted you to know that I've kept my word —
don't worry — poetry is making a wonderful ruin of me.
Flowers are sprouting out of this parched ground.

Rachael Boast

THE EARTH HOUSE

I would have me an earth house, an earth house,
With roots above my head,
Like a cailleach's hair they'd thatch my lair,
This dwelling, to Darkness wed.

Here, Winter would not enter
Not one high word be said
Where, deep and whole with the tunnelling mole
I'd have me a mossy bed.

Out of the way of the adder,
The stoat and the pecking crow,
No storm would ever find me,
No blustery breezes blow.

And warm in the land of shadows
With roots I'd wrap me round,
Deep in the forest's fabric
In the house in the quiet ground.

I'd turn my cheek to the willow
And words from my mouth would spill
And the busy world stop turning
And with peace my bones would fill.

Sheena Blackhall

IT WAS LIKE THIS: YOU WERE HAPPY

It was like this:
you were happy, then you were sad,
then happy again, then not.

It went on.
You were innocent or you were guilty.
Actions were taken, or not.

At times you spoke, at other times you were silent.
Mostly, it seems you were silent — what could you say?

Now it is almost over.

Like a lover, your life bends down and kisses your life.

It does this not in forgiveness —
between you, there is nothing to forgive —
but with the simple nod of a baker at the moment
he sees the bread is finished with transformation.

Eating, too, is a thing now only for others.

It doesn't matter what they will make of you
or your days: they will be wrong,
they will miss the wrong woman, miss the wrong man,
all the stories they tell will be tales of their own invention.

Your story was this: you were happy, then you were sad,
you slept, you awakened.
Sometimes you ate roasted chestnuts, sometimes persimmons.

Jane Hirshfield

ADVICE TO SELF

What if it all ends?
Let it end — let the sand win.
Sky and earth go on.

Olga Kenyon

ABOUT THE CONTRIBUTORS

Anne Aylor's novel, *Angel Hotel*, was published in the US and UK and she has recently completed her second, *The Double Happiness Company*. She is the founder of Ulysses' Cave which offers creative writing courses in the UK and abroad and loves to write because it doesn't involve high math or high heels.

Sheena Blackhall is a Scots writer, storyteller, illustrator and traditional ballad singer. From 1998-2003 she was Creative Writing Fellow in Scots at Aberdeen University's Elphinstone Institute. She has published 2 Scots novellas, 10 short story collections, and 40 volumes of poetry. Two plays have been televised. She has won many national awards for her writing in Scots.

Rachael Boast was born in Suffolk, England, in 1975. After completing a degree in English and Philosophy she moved to Bristol and began self-publishing. The work that appears here is from two collections: *Dancing on Ice* (2002) and *The Gaps in Tangled Grass* (2002).

Jen Brown has been writing poetry since her teens and has attended many writing retreats (run by Wolf at The Door). She lives in a garret in Bristol, England and manages a bookshop for Oxfam. The poems that appear here are from her self-published collection *Puzzle*.

Larry Butler was born in the USA and has lived in Glasgow since 1981, teaching Tai-Chi, movement and creative writing. His poems and articles have appeared in numerous magazines. A co-founder of the Poetry Healing Project, he developed Survivors' Poetry Scotland and is presently involved in making an arts/eco-village and collaborating with a jeweller, a visual artist and an architect to make a portable, autonomous, origami hut!

Mary Clark (Amarapuspa) works in a Buddhist women's wholefood business in Croydon, England, and enjoys writing in her limited free time. She is originally from New York and was greatly affected by the events of 11th September.

Alison Clayburn lives in London by the Thames. After a long career as a community worker she became an adult educator, specialising in creative writing for personal development. She describes herself as a `writing groupie' and gains much from residential courses, writing retreats and workshops.

Pam Cooper was born in Staffordshire, in 1954. She has written poetry most of her life, worked as a literacy teacher, and been a practising Buddhist for over twenty years. She currently lives in Hove, on the South Coast of England.

Dhruvasimha was born in Hartlepool, Co. Durham, England, in 1938. He was a radio officer in the Merchant Navy 1956-1961 and then worked in commercial television studios for the next 30 years. He has retired to Whitby in Yorkshire where he writes, practises geology and genealogy, and makes enamel pictures by fusing glass onto copper.

Terry Diffey lectured in philosophy, specialising in aesthetics, at the University of Sussex before he retired in 2003. He has published poems in *Doors, South, The Powys Review, Urthona* and the FWBO anthology, *Letting the Silence Speak*. He has participated in the Brighton Buddhist Centre (England) since 1984.

Linda France has published four collections with Bloodaxe Books. The latest is *The Simultaneous Dress* (2002). Her verse biography of Lady Mary Wortley Montagu *The Toast of the Kit Cat Club* is due from Bloodaxe in 2005. She edited the acclaimed anthology *Sixty Women Poets* in 1993 and writes a regular feature on the craft of poetry for *Mslexia* magazine. She has worked on 20 Public Art collaborations since 1990. *Diamonds in Your Pockets* and *I am Frida Kahlo* were commissions for the stage in 1996 and 2002. Linda is currently working on her first novel. She lives in the north of England.

Jeremy Glenn is a Montana native, where for several years he worked in the Buddhist-run East Indian café, Tipu's Tiger. He recently received a degree in Creative Writing from the University of Montana, and was last seen headed on a three month pilgrimage of India and Nepal.

Sam Hamill has published more than forty books, including translations from Greek, Latin, Chinese and Japanese. He co-founded and was Editor at Copper Canyon Press for 32 years, and is Founder and Director of Poets Against War. His selected poems and translations, *Almost Paradise*, was recently published by Shambhala.

Graham Hartill lives in the Black Mountains, where he runs writing workshops, particularly in the fields of health care and mental health. He has received several arts council fellowships and worked until recently for the Ledbury Poetry Festival as Lifelines Co-ordinator with elders throughout Herefordshire. His selected poems, *Cennau's Bell*, is out this year.

Jane Hirshfield, a practitioner of Soto Zen since 1974, is the author of five books of poetry, most recently *Given Sugar, Given Salt* (NY: HarperCollins, 2001), and a collection of essays, *Nine Gates: Entering The Mind of Poetry* (NY: HarperCollins, 1997). Her honours include fellowships from the Guggenheim and Rockefeller Foundations, awards from The Poetry Center, The Poetry Society of America, the California Book Award, and others. Her collection *Each Happiness Ringed by Lions: Selected Poems* is published by Bloodaxe Books, (2005).

Alastair Jessiman (Sarvananda) was born in Glasgow in 1958 and moved to Norwich after his ordination in 1987. Since then he has worked for Norwich

Buddhist Centre and been the Buddhist chaplain to Norwich prison. He is currently writing a radio and a stage play. His first radio play, *Star Man* was broadcast on Radio 4 in 2004.

Thomas Jones (Dhivan) started writing seriously in 1996 after a month's solitary retreat in the Scottish Highlands. Since then he's written poems, short stories and novels. He is also involved with editing Urthona, the magazine of Buddhism and the arts. The poems that appear here are from two self-published collections *Haera*, and *Glen Affric Poems*.

David Keefe (Manjusvara) lives in Bristol where he edits Weatherlight Press, publishing American Poetry in the UK, and co-leads (with Ananda) the popular Wolf at the Door writing workshops. He has had poetry and essays published in Britain and America, and his book *Writing Your Way* was published by Windhorse in Spring 2005.

Olga Kenyon had three sons and is sorry not to have discovered Buddhism then, to create a better home. She has taught French, lectured in Spanish and written too many books on women's writing, from *Women Novelists Today* (Harvester), and *800 Years of Women's Letters* (Sutton), to *Introduction to Black Women Novelists*.

Ko Un was born in 1933 in Kunsan, North Cholla Province and is Korea's foremost living writer. After immense suffering during the Korean War, he became a Buddhist monk. His first poems were published in 1958, while he was the disciple of a great Master, the Venerable Hyobong. A few years later he returned to the world and became a leading spokesman in the struggle for freedom and democracy during the 1970s and 1980s, in a struggle for which he was often arrested and imprisoned. He has published more than 120 volumes of poems, essays, and fiction. In recent years, selections from his work have been translated into at least fourteen languages. *1000 Lives* (selection; published by Green Integer) will be out in Autumn 2005.

[Ko Un's Translators: **Brother Anthony of Taizé** is a professor in the English Department at Sogang University, Seoul, where he has been teaching Medieval and Renaissance English literature and culture since the 1980s. He is a leading translator of Korean literature. Born in England, he is now a Korean national with the name An Sonjae. The late **Young-moo Kim**, (1944-2002) was a Professor of English Literature at Seoul National University, and was well known in Korea as a literary critic and poet. He published three volumes of his own poetry. **Gary G. Gach** is a poet, translator and writer living in San Francisco. He is the author of *The Complete Idiot's Guide to Understanding Buddhism* and edited the Buddhist poetry anthology *What Book?* for Parallax Press.]

Julia Lewis lives in London in a Buddhist women's community, and her poems have been widely published (*PN Review; Poetry London, Enitharmon Press*) and performed. In 2004, she won first prize in the Poetry London competition, and was commended in the National Poetry competition 2005.

Grevel Lindop works in Manchester as a freelance writer. Books include *Selected Poems* (2000), *Touching the Earth* (2001: a poem-in-progress on the life of the Buddha), and *Playing With Fire* (Carcanet, forthcoming 2006). He has practised and sometimes taught Buddhist meditation with the Samatha Trust.

Maitreyabandhu was born in 1961 and lives and works at the London Buddhist Centre in the East End of London. He divides his time between teaching and writing. His first book *Thicker than Blood: Friendship on the Buddhist Path* (Windhorse Publications) was published in 2001.

Michael McClure has published more than thirty books of poetry and prose and is one of the founding figures of the San Francisco Renaissance and the Beat Generation. Recently he has published two CDs, one with The Doors' keyboardist Ray Manzarek, *There's a Word* and the other a collaboration with composer Terry Riley, *I Like your eyes Liberty*. His most recent book is *Plum Stones: Cartoons of No Heaven*. McClure lives in the Oakland Hills with sculptor Amy Evans McClure.

Tony McKeown was born in Belfast in 1971. Moving first to Dublin then London, he studied philosophy at Middlesex University.

Andrew Miller was born in 1966 and lives in Leeds, UK. Of himself, he says 'I am an incurable romantic and optimist. I believe in the power of love and creativity to transform any situation. I often find the world a baffling and painful place. I meditate and write poetry to keep myself sane.'

Simon Millward works for a national charity and lives in the countryside outside Nottingham, England. A lover of poetry and the natural world, he regularly attends writing retreats with Wolf at the Door, and has had poems published in a number of booklets and magazines.

Padmakara (Roger Bygott) was Ordained into the Western Buddhist Order in 1991 and has moved through many landscapes and lifestyles from community life in Bristol, monasticism in the mountains of Spain, to solitude in the valleys of North Wales. He currently lives with his girlfriend on the edge of Saddleworth Moor in northern England. The poems that appear here are from his self-published collection *Always more Apples: Selected Poems 1998-2000* (Pole Star Press 2002).

Stephen Parr (Ananda) was born in 1944 in Blackburn, Lancashire. He has written both fiction and poetry, his poems having appeared in many journals and in Bloodaxe's anthology *The Long Pale Corridor*. They have also been broadcast on BBC Radio. Since 1996 he has been co-leader of Wolf at the Door, which runs Buddhist-inspired writing workshops around the world. He has produced numerous poetry collections, and in 1999 his full-length poetry collection *North of the Future* was published by Windhorse.

David Penn was born in north Kent. He now lives in south London while being involved with the West London Buddhist Centre. His poetry has appeared in *Magma*, *Urthona* and *Smith's Knoll* and his first published short story appeared in 2004.

Bruce Peterkin was born in Edinburgh in 1967, and brought up in a small town in East Lothian, Scotland. He lives in a Buddhist men's community in Norwich, and spends time with his son Nat (12) and partner, Satyagita. He works as a web-developer. He attended a writing group for 4 years and produced a novel.

Tony Press (Acarasiddhi) lives in San Francisco and loves teaching English to newly-arrived immigrant high school students. Prior to teaching, he was a criminal defence attorney. He is now struggling to complete a set of short stories. He first meditated in 1991. He was ordained into the Western Buddhist Order in February 2005.

Ratnagarbha (Ambrose Gilson) lives in Cambridge UK, where he runs *Urthona*, the Buddhist arts magazine. Between phone calls he reads Neruda and Nietzsche and is writing a novel about Cambridge as it might be three hundred years in the future.

Saddhanandi began attending the Glasgow Buddhist Centre in 1983. In 1994 her Buddhist practice deepened whilst nursing her father through terminal cancer; a year later she was ordained. She is now Chairwoman of Taraloka, a women's Buddhist Retreat Centre, and remains inspired by human potential and the possibility of Enlightenment.

Sangharakshita was ordained as a monk in India in 1950, and returned to England in 1964 where in 1967 he founded a new Buddhist movement, the Friends of the Western Buddhist Order, which now has centres worldwide. One of his many preoccupations has been the connection between the Arts and the Spiritual Life. He has himself been a prolific writer of both prose and poetry, and his *Complete Poems 1941/1994* was published by Windhorse Publications in 1995.

Sasanaratna (Derek Goodman) was born in Glasgow in 1959. He has been practising Buddhism since 1977 and now lives in Edinburgh. His main literary influence comes from the French Symbolist/Surrealist tradition and his poetry is often concerned with the mystery and paradox of human desire.

Satyadaka was born in Wanstead Hospital in 1960, and grew up under another name that he still retains for legal purposes. Besides poems he has written an autobiography, as yet unpublished. He is a keen performer of his own and others' work, and also likes to play the saxophone. He lives in Norwich, UK. The poem that appears here is from his self-published collection *The Truth of Love*.

Linda Saunders' poems have been widely published in magazines and anthologies in the UK, including *New Women Poets* from Bloodaxe Books. Her recent full-length collection, *Ways of Returning*, is published by Arrowhead Press, following an introductory selection, *She River*, from Vane Women Press, 1999.

Henry Shukman won the Daily Telegraph Arvon Prize in 2000, and has received awards from the Arts Council of England and Southern Arts. His first work of fiction, *Darien Dogs*, was published by Jonathan Cape in 2004, and his first collection of poetry *In Doctor No's Garden*, also published by Jonathan Cape, was a Book of the Year in the Times and Guardian, was short listed for the Forward Prize and won the Aldeburgh Prize in 2002. He has worked as a travel writer, and sometimes writes for the *New York Times Book Review*.

Thomas R. Smith is a poet, editor, and teacher living in western Wisconsin. He has published three acclaimed books of poetry, *Keeping the Star* (1988), *Horse of Earth* (1994), and *The Dark Indigo Current* (2000). He edited a US selection of the Canadian poet Alden Nowlan, *What Happened When he Went to the Store for Bread*. During 2004, he published a chapbook called *Peace Vigil: Poems for an election year (and after)*.

Srivati writes poetry (and the occasional piece of prose or play) because it renders life more vivid and meaningful, and because then she feels more like herself, even though she doesn't really know who exactly that might be. She lives in London.

Subhadassi was born in Huddersfield in 1967. He was ordained into the Western Buddhist Order in 1992. His chapbook *Sublunary Voodoo* was published by Mudfog in 1998. The full-length collection *peeled* was published by Arc in 2004. Its title poem received a special commendation in the 2005 Forward Prize.

Ian Tromp (Manjusura) was born and grew up in Johannesburg, South Africa. He writes poetry, short fiction, and essays. He has published one volume of poems, *Setting Out,* and co-edited a South African poetry anthology, *The Heart In Exile* (Penguin, 1996). He presently lives in Birmingham.

Duncan Tweedale was born Rochdale, Lancashire in 1943. Now in Bath, thankfully retired. Practising in the Thai forest tradition of Theravadin Buddhism since 1980s, though some of the poems selected predate this. He is editor of *Bath Dharma Journal* for the Bath Buddhist Group, which includes followers of a wide range of Buddhist traditions.

Chase Twichell has published five books of poetry, the most recent of which is *The Snow Watcher* (Ontario Review Press, 1998 and Bloodaxe, 1999). A new book o poems, *Dog Language* is forthcoming from Copper Canyon Press in 2005. She is also the translator, with Tony K. Stewart, of *The Lover of God* by Rabindranath Tagore (Copper Canyon, 2004) and co-editor of *The Practice of poetry: Writing Exercises from Poets Who Teach* (HarperCollins). In 1999 she quit teaching (at Princeton University) to start Ausable Press, which publishes contemporary poetry.

Varasahaya ('noble friend') has been a Buddhist for 14 years. After completing a degree in law she incarnated as a youth worker, interpersonal skills trainer and masseuse. She works at Birmingham Buddhist Centre and lives with her partner and two children. Loves are Wales, walking, gardening, ritual and her friends.

Michael Venditozzi was born in Toronto, Canada in 1971. He was brought up in Scotland and has lived in Glasgow, London, and Paris. He is now a member of the Western Buddhist Order and lives and works in Cambridge. For the past two years his poems have been published regularly in *Agenda* magazine.

Jayne Wilding has been practicing with the Sakya school for some years. Her first collection *In The Moon's Pantry* is being published by Diehard, Scotland. Recently she has worked as a Renga Master at the Tramway Theatre, Glasgow – helping create linked haiku in the Secret Garden.

CREDITS

Thanks are due to the following authors and publishers for giving their permission to republish here: Sheena Blackhall: 'Midgie Matrix & Incantation' from *The Dule Tree*, 2004 (Finavon Print and Design in association with the Elphinstone Institute, Aberdeen University), and 'The Styx flows through Balquhidder' from a limited edition poetry volume *The Boddamer's Monkey; Place Poems in Scots & English* (Thistle Reprographics, Aberdeen 2004). Also to *Poetry Scotland*. Sam Hamill: 'The Orchid Flower' is from *Dumb Luck* (BOA Editions, 2002); 'Summer Rain' is from *Almost Paradise: New & Selected Poems & Translations* (Shambhala, Spring 2005). Graham Hartill: 'Pictish Stones' was first published in *Open World*, Glasgow in 1991. Jane Hirshfield: 'The Heart as Origami' from *The October Palace* (NY: HarperCollins, 1994), © 1994 Jane Hirshfield, used by permission of Harper Collins. 'The Heart's Counting Knows Only One' from *The Lives of the Heart* (NY: HarperCollins, 1997), © 1997 Jane Hirshfield, used by permission of Harper Collins. 'Tree and Habit' from *Given Sugar, Given Salt* (NY: HarperCollins, 2001),© 2001 Jane Hirshfield, used by permission of HarperCollins. 'It Was Like This: You Were Happy' and 'The Monk Stood Beside a Wheelbarrow' from *After*, (NY: HarperCollins, 2006); © 2003, 2004, 2005, 2006, Jane Hirshfield, used by permission of Jane Hirshfield. David Keefe (Manjusvara): 'Ghazal (Buddha)' has already appeared in the *1997 FWBO Anthology*, and 'Edinburgh Airport' was included in the *2000 FWBO Anthology* (Rising Fire Press). 'Words for Jacob' was originally published in *Jefferson Monthly*. 'Edinburgh Airport in *Edinburgh: An Intimate City*. Ko Un: 'A Drunkard', 'Dayfly', 'A Friend', and 'A Worm', all previously appeared in *Beyond Self* published by Parallax Press (currently out of print). Julia Lewis: 'Trees', 'The Miracle' appeared in *PN Review*; and *Entering the Tapestry*, Enitharmon Press; 'Nasturtium Leaves', and 'Same Chair Same Window' were published by *Poetry London*, and 'Dream of the Singing Graveyard', *Urthona*, 2004. Grevel Lindop: 'Scattering the Ashes' first appeared in *PN Review*. Stephen Parr (Ananda): 'Aquae Sulis', 'Meaning', 'Going Home' and 'Clematis' are all from *North of The Future* (Windhorse Publications); Linda Saunders: 'Stranger in Sydney Gardens' and 'Midwinter Birch Tree' are included in Linda Saunders' collection *Ways of Returning*, Arrowhead Press, 2004. 'Without Skylarks', 'Poet's Whistle' and 'Stranger in Sydney Gardens' appeared in *Urthona*, Winter 2004. Padmakara: 'Horizons' was published in *Urthona* (Autumn 2001).

Sangharakshita: 'Sequence in a Strange Land', 'Petals', 'In the Woods are Many More', and 'Haiku', are all from *Sangharakshita: The Complete Poems 1941/1994* (Windhorse Publications, 1995). 'The Call of the Forest' is the title poem of a subsequent collection, and again is reprinted with the permission of Windhorse, (2000). Sasanaratna: 'The End of the Sentence', was first published in *FWBO New Poetry 2000*, Rising Fire Press. Henry Shukman: 'Snowy Morning' and 'Horses at Christmas' are from *In Doctor No's Garden* published by Jonathan Cape, 2002, used by permission of The Random House Group Limited. Subhadassi: 'Dakini over New York' and 'Birds' were both published in *peeled*, ARC press, 2004. Ian Tromp (Manjusura): 'That Summer' was first published in *PN Review*, and subsequently in *FWBO New Poetry 2000* (Rising Fire Press). Duncan Tweedale: All of the poems were published in *The Collector of Jade* (Wolf at the Door Limited Editions, 1999). The poems 'As Josquin Would' and 'The Collector of Jade' were first published in *Poetry Wales*, and 'The Spoils' in *Other Poetry*. Chase Twichell: 'Glimpse', 'Pine', 'Tea Mind', 'Weightless like a River', and 'The Year I got rid of Everything' are from *The Snow Watcher* (Ontario Review Press, Princeton NJ, 1998 and Bloodaxe, 1999). Michael Venditozzi (Candradasa): 'Asking for Rain' was first published in *Agenda*, 2004. Jayne Wilding: 'Arrive in Dehradun' and 'Beyond the Village' are soon to appear in her first collection *In The Moon's Pantry* published by Diehard, Scotland.